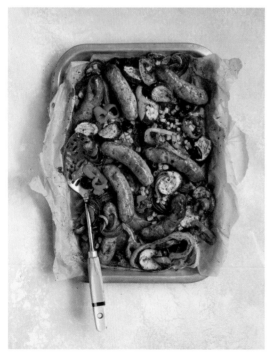

DINNER'S
IN THE BAG

LOUISE KENNEY

Photography by Ola Smit

Hardie Grant

QUADRILLE

Publishing Director Sarah Lavelle
Editor Harriet Webster
Copy Editor Samantha Stanley
Designer Katherine Keeble
Photographer Ola Smit
Food Stylist Louise Kenney
Production Director Vincent Smith
Production Controller Katie Jarvis

First published in 2019 by Quadrille,
an imprint of Hardie Grant Publishing

Quadrille
52–54 Southwark Street
London SE1 1UN
quadrille.com

Cataloguing in Publication Data: a catalogue record for this
book is available from the British Library.

ISBN: 978 1 78713 485 0

Printed in China

CONTENTS

—

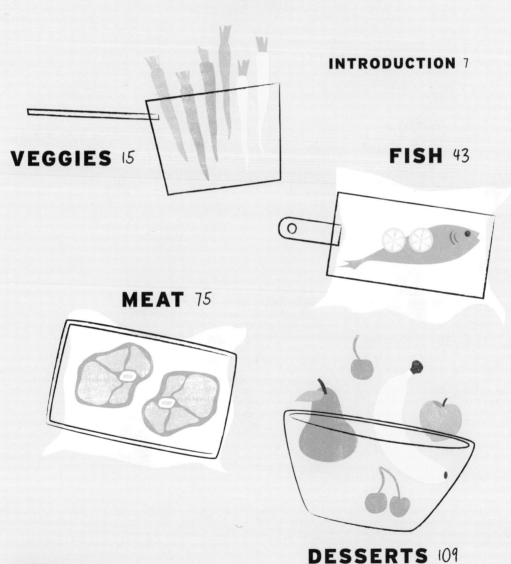

Introduction

Dinner's ready and it's in the (oven) bag, or parchment or foil parcel... If you have any of these three items in your kitchen, and if you lack the time and energy to slave over a hot stove every day, then this book is definitely for you. I am an impatient cook and my guess is there are lots of you out there just like me, so throughout the following pages you will find recipes that are tasty, unfussy, require no stove preparation and produce very little washing up.

Cooking in this way means you can prepare your meal, bung it in the oven, set the timer and then wander off to do something else. This is the ultimate in lazy cooking (and my favourite method when I am tired during a hectic week). It means you can put your feet up to watch some telly or get back to finishing off your work, or entertain your guests as they arrive, safe in the knowledge that something delicious is cooking away.

If you haven't cooked in this way before then I would suggest you start with the following recipes to build up your confidence. I have chosen them because they are fast, very easy to prepare and look impressive when dished up.

The term *en papillotte* is traditionally used to describe food that is cooked and served in parchment paper or foil. The paper is wrapped around the food then tightly sealed, so all the ingredients are completely enclosed. This method is fantastic for keeping moisture inside the parcel, thereby retaining the natural juices of the ingredients. It's also great for those who loathe washing up! It's an ideal method for busy families, housemates and singles who just want a nice dinner without the faff. Almost all of the recipes can be reduced to serve one, or doubled, to suit your needs.

Each recipe requires parchment, foil or an oven or Stasher bag (see page 12), and the best method is indicated in the photo and text, but you'll see from the handy illustrations at the bottom of each recipe that the materials are interchangeable, so fear not if you only have foil or parchment to hand – you'll still be able to cook most of the recipes hassle- and mess-free.

Now, how on earth do you make a parchment parcel? There are several ways to wrap up food for cooking but the scrunch and twist method is my preferred way – mostly because it's not too fiddly. See the pictures on pages 10 and 11 for more help. First, you need to cut a piece of greaseproof or parchment paper large enough to contain all the ingredients with plenty of paper to spare around the edges. Do check each recipe, though, as some, like the Seafood pasta (on page 63) have individual parcels for each guest.

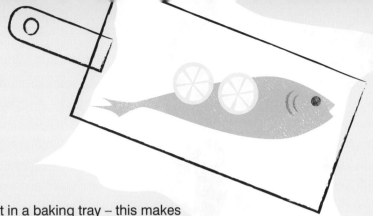

Next, place the parchment in a baking tray – this makes it easier to transfer in and out of the oven – then pile on the ingredients. Bring the short sides of the paper together and fold over two or three times, making sure you leave some space above the food for the air to circulate. You will have a hollow tube-like structure. Next, twist one end of the paper tightly and repeat with the other end to completely seal the food inside. Once the food is cooked, take good care when opening up your parcel as lots of steam can escape and has the potential to burn you.

I like to use compostable parchment and greaseproof paper, which are available to buy online and in whole food stores – also look out for unbleached greaseproof or parchment paper. Siliconised baking paper is not compostable so bear that in mind if you'd like to be zero waste in the kitchen. You can also buy reusable parchment sealed with cooking clips but none of these recipes have been tested using this method. If you have a go, let me know how you get on!

A foil parcel is almost the same as using parchment but it is much easier to close. Follow the steps as for parchment paper but simply scrunch the ends together instead of twisting them. When a recipe calls for the parcel to be opened up then sealed again, take care to not to rip the foil, as it tends to be more fragile than paper and harder to close back up tightly.

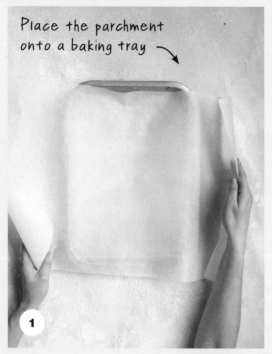

Place the parchment onto a baking tray

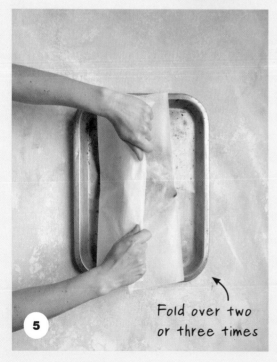

Fold over two or three times

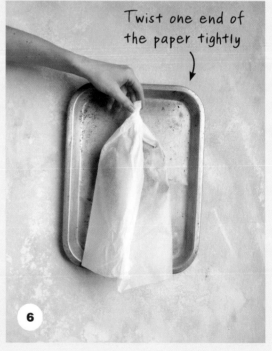

Twist one end of the paper tightly

3

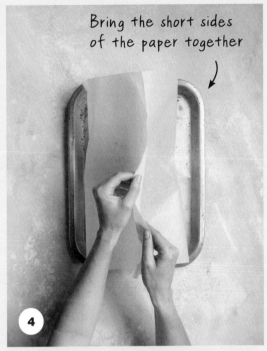

Bring the short sides
of the paper together

4

Repeat with
the other end

7

8

Oven bags are a cinch. I used Bacofoil and Reynolds oven bags when I was writing this book, and they are so easy to use, but other brands are available. Each packet comes with instructions on the back. If you run out of the ties, you can happily use cook's string instead. When using bags, unlike with parchment or foil, make sure you cut 4–6 little slits in the top of the bag (under the tie) to allow the steam to escape during cooking. Oven bags are excellent for the recipes with lots of stock or water in them and, being transparent, you can see what is happening to your food as it cooks – mesmerising!

An alternative to all of the above is a Stasher bag. These are washable, reusable oven and freezer pockets, and they are fantastic if you want to cook small amounts of food – definitely a good purchase if there are 1–2 of you to cook for and perfect if you want to reduce what you chuck in the bin. I bought mine online but you can find them in most good kitchen shops.

One last thing to remember – baking trays are essential for this type of cooking. They make transferring your parcels in and out of the oven a breeze. Some trays will need to be deep-sided and others simply flat. I have indicated what is best for each recipe but use your own judgement based on what you are cooking.

Happy lazy cooking and eating!

VEGGIES

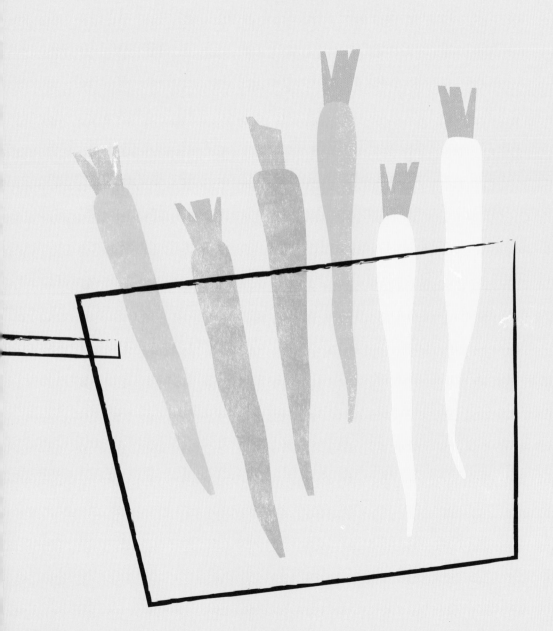

Ratatouille

This is a chunky version of the traditional ratatouille but requires minimal effort. It's lovely served with crispy baked potatoes and lashings of butter or olive oil. This recipe is vegan but is also yummy served with grated Parmesan.

1 Preheat the oven to 180°C fan (400°F/Gas 6). Line a baking dish with a sheet of parchment, two sheets of foil, or a large oven bag.

2 Put the aubergine pieces into a colander. Sprinkle with salt and set aside. Score a cross into each tomato, pop them into a heatproof bowl and cover with boiling water. Leave for 10 minutes then peel away the skin and slice each tomato in half.

3 Add the tomatoes, onion, courgette, pepper, sun-blush tomatoes and garlic to the lined baking dish. Rinse the salt off the aubergine pieces, pat dry with kitchen paper and place on top of the other veg. Mix well.

4 Season everything well, pour over the olive oil and balsamic vinegar and tuck in the thyme and rosemary sprigs. Seal the parcel (see pages 10–11). (If using an oven bag, snip a few slits in the top to allow steam to escape.)

5 Bake in the oven for 40–50 minutes. Remove from the oven and rest for 10 minutes before dishing up with the basil scattered over.

1 medium aubergine (eggplant) cut into 2-cm (¾-in) chunks
6 medium sized ripe tomatoes
1 large red onion, cut into 1-cm (½-in) wedges
1 medium courgette (zucchini) cut into 2-cm (¾-in) chunks
1 red (bell) pepper, deseeded and cut into thick strips
8 large sun-blush tomatoes, chopped into pieces
2 garlic cloves, finely sliced
2 tbsp extra virgin olive oil
2 tbsp balsamic vinegar
2 sprigs of thyme
2 sprigs of rosemary
salt and freshly ground black pepper

To serve
1 small bunch of basil, leaves chopped or left whole

Serves 4–6

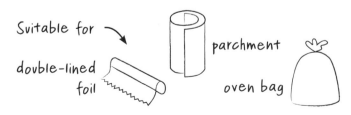

Suitable for →
double-lined foil
parchment
oven bag

Whole baked mushrooms with spinach and cream

Baked mushrooms make a satisfying meal and they're super easy to whip up. This serves three people for an easy supper, or six as a starter. Cooking them *en papillotte* means they stay nice and juicy.

1 Preheat the oven to 180°C fan (400°F/Gas 6). Line a baking dish with two sheets of foil or parchment.

2 Mix the shallot, garlic and tarragon with the oil in a bowl and season generously with salt and pepper.

3 Put the baby spinach in a thick layer on the bottom of the lined baking dish, top with the mushrooms (gill side up) and season with salt and pepper. Spoon the shallot mixture over each mushroom, then pour over the cream, close up the parcel tightly (see pages 10–11) and transfer to the oven to bake for 40 minutes.

4 After 40 minutes has elapsed, open up the parcel, scatter over the pine nuts and bake, uncovered, for another 5 minutes.

5 Remove from the oven and grate over as much Parmesan as you like. Serve immediately with some crusty bread.

1 banana shallot,
    finely chopped
1 garlic clove, finely chopped
1 tbsp finely chopped
    fresh tarragon
1 tbsp extra virgin olive oil
100g (3½oz) baby spinach
6 large Portobello mushrooms
150ml (⅔ cup) double
    (heavy) cream
2 tbsp pine nuts
salt and freshly ground
    black pepper

To serve
Parmesan
plenty of crusty bread

Serves 3 as a light main
or 6 as a starter

Suitable for

double-lined
    foil

double-lined
parchment

Baked peppers with lentils and goat's cheese

Nutty lentils with creamy goat's cheese encased in a soft, sweet red pepper – divine! This makes great camping food as it works well cooked in foil in the embers of an open fire.

1 Preheat the oven to 200°C fan (425°F/Gas 7). Cut 4 sheets of baking parchment or foil.

2 Cut the 'lid' off the peppers, keeping the stalk on, about 1cm (½ in) down from the top. Remove the seeds and white pith. Arrange a pepper, cut side up, with its lid, cut side down, onto each piece of parchment. Drizzle with a little olive oil and season generously with salt and pepper. Close up the parcels (see pages 10–11), sit them on a baking dish and bake in the oven for 25 minutes.

3 Meanwhile, prepare the filling in a bowl: crumble the goat's cheese, add the Puy lentils, sun-blush tomatoes, lemon zest and herbs. Season generously with salt, drizzle over ½ a tablespoon of olive oil and stir to combine everything together.

4 Remove the peppers from the oven and carefully open up the parchment – they should be soft but still holding their shape. Stuff the filling into each pepper and put the lid on top. Gently close up the parchment and return to the oven for 10 minutes.

5 Remove from the oven and place the parcels straight onto plates. Pull open the parchment and sprinkle over the flaked almonds to serve.

4 red (bell) peppers
olive oil, for drizzling
125g (4½oz) fresh
 goat's cheese
1 x 250-g (9-oz) packet
 ready-cooked Puy lentils
6 sun-blush tomatoes,
 each cut into 2 or 3 pieces
finely grated zest of 1 lemon
½ small bunch of flat leaf
 parsley, finely chopped
leaves from 3 stalks of
 oregano, finely chopped
a few fennel fronds,
 finely chopped
a small handful of toasted
 flaked (slivered) almonds
salt and freshly ground
 black pepper

Serves 4

Suitable for

foil

parchment

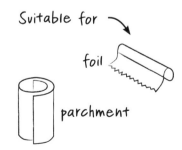

Warm potato salad
with roasted garlic

What could be better than warm potatoes with creamy garlic and mayonnaise? Whenever I make this dish, it gets eaten up and there are never any leftovers. This works really well served alongside the Roast chicken with fennel on page 93. If you'd like to make your mayonnaise vegan, substitute a block of silken tofu for the egg yolks and use a stick blender or a small food processor instead of a whisk.

1 Preheat the oven to 200°C fan (425°F/Gas 7). Line a baking dish with a large piece of parchment or foil, or an oven bag.

2 Spread the potatoes in the lined baking dish, drizzle over the olive oil and season with salt and pepper. Nestle the whole garlic bulb in between the potatoes. Seal up the parcel (see pages 10–11) and bake in the oven for 1 hour. (If using an oven bag, snip a few slits in the top to allow steam to escape.)

3 Meanwhile, make the mayonnaise. Put the egg yolks, mustard and vinegar into a mixing bowl and season with salt and pepper. Using an electric or balloon whisk, whisk briefly then gradually pour in the olive oil and sunflower oil, whisking as you go until the sauce thickens. Taste and adjust the seasoning. Add a little more vinegar if required then stir in the chives, mint and dill. Set aside until the potatoes are cooked.

4 Remove the potatoes from the oven. Open the parcel and lift out the garlic bulb. Let it cool slightly then squeeze the garlic cloves out of their skins onto the potatoes. Gently crush the potatoes and garlic together with a fork. Tip into a serving bowl and stir in the herby mayonnaise. Serve warm.

1kg (2lb 4oz) red-skinned
  new potatoes, washed
1 tbsp olive oil
1 whole garlic bulb
salt and freshly ground
  black pepper

For the mayonnaise
2 egg yolks
1 tsp Dijon mustard
2 tsp apple cider vinegar
  or white wine vinegar
100ml (generous ⅓ cup)
  extra virgin olive oil
120ml (½ cup) sunflower oil
1 tbsp chopped chives
1 tbsp chopped mint leaves
1 tbsp chopped dill

Serves 4 generously

Suitable for

foil

parchment

oven bag

Corn on the cob with chilli, mayonnaise and lime

I first came across this combination of flavours when I was travelling and working in Oaxaca, Mexico. You could buy corn at the vegetable market, barbecued on a wooden skewer, slathered in mayonnaise, hot chilli powder and lime. It was a revelation (along with so many other flavours which were brand-new to me) and I've never forgotten it. You could easily dispense with the parchment paper and make this recipe on the barbecue – roast the corn directly over the hot coals until charred then add butter and the remaining ingredients.

1 Preheat the oven to 200°C fan (425°F/Gas 7). Line a baking dish with a large piece of parchment or foil, or an oven bag.

2 Arrange the cobs in a single layer in the lined baking dish, dot over the butter and sprinkle generously with sea salt. Close up the parcel (see pages 10–11) and bake in the oven for 20 minutes. (If using an oven bag, snip a few slits in the top to allow steam to escape.) Open up the parcel so all of the corn cobs are exposed, baste each one in the buttery juices and return to the oven, uncovered, for another 20 minutes.

3 Remove from the oven, baste again with the juices, slather mayonnaise over each corn cob, then sprinkle with cayenne pepper. Squeeze over the lime juice and sprinkle over the zest, then season with more sea salt and eat immediately.

4 corn on the cob,
  husks removed
30g (2 tbsp) salted butter
4 tbsp mayonnaise,
  plus extra if you're feeling
  greedy (see page 23 for
  homemade)
½ tsp cayenne pepper
zest and juice of 1 lime
sea salt

Serves 4

Suitable for

foil

parchment

oven bag

Aubergine with miso, ginger, pak choi and spring onions

This is a light, healthy veggie dish that yields soft and flavourful aubergine. Best made with aubergines when they're in season during the summer and early autumn months. You could substitute pak choi for shredded Chinese cabbage, but halve the amount of boiling water and the cooking time to 5 minutes.

1 Preheat the oven to 190°C fan (410°F/Gas 6–7). Line a baking dish with parchment or foil, big enough to fit all the aubergine halves, and another sheet of parchment or foil on a separate baking dish for the pak choi.

2 Using a small sharp knife, score the aubergine flesh in a crisscross pattern then sit on the lined baking dish, cut side up.

3 Mix the ginger, garlic, sesame oil, chilli flakes, miso and honey together in a bowl. Season with salt and pepper (sparingly as some miso can be very salty), then spread this over the cut side of the aubergines. Carefully close up the parcel (see pages 10–11), leaving room for the air to circulate inside. Bake for 40 minutes.

4 Towards the end of the 40 minutes, prepare the pak choi – separate out the leaves and wash them. Shake off any excess water, then pile the leaves in a heap onto the second lined baking dish. Drizzle over the soy sauce and carefully pour over the boiling water. Seal the parcel tightly and bake in the oven for 10 minutes.

5 At the same time, lift out the aubergine parcel, open it up and return to the oven to brown for 15 minutes.

6 Remove both parcels from the oven and serve each aubergine half with some pak choi leaves, sprinkled with the spring onions and cashews.

2 medium aubergines (eggplants), halved lengthways
2-cm (¾-in) piece of fresh ginger, peeled and finely diced
1 garlic clove, grated or crushed
1 tbsp toasted sesame oil
1 tsp dried chilli flakes
1 tbsp brown rice miso paste
2 tbsp runny honey
3 heads pak choi, leaves separated
½ tbsp light soy sauce
100ml (generous ½ cup) boiling water
salt and freshly ground black pepper

To serve
½ bunch of spring onions (scallions), finely sliced
a small handful of cashews, roughly chopped

Serves 2

Suitable for

foil

parchment

Baked sweet potatoes with goat's cheese, parsley and lemon

This is a great recipe for outdoor cooking – perfect for barbecuing or cooking in foil in the embers of an open fire. If you want to 'meatify' this recipe, add some thick slices of chorizo to the lentils just before popping back into the oven.

1 Preheat the oven to 200°C fan (425°F/Gas 7). Line a baking dish with parchment or foil, or an oven bag.

2 Place your sweet potatoes in the lined dish. Seal up the parcel tightly (see pages 10–11) and bake in the oven for an hour. (If using an oven bag, snip a few slits in the top to allow steam to escape.)

3 Meanwhile, mix the lentils with most of the parsley, the chilli flakes, coriander seeds, lemon zest and juice and a little olive oil in a bowl and season with salt and pepper.

4 Remove the potatoes from the oven, carefully unwrap, but keep them in their parcel. Cut almost in half, drizzle over a little olive oil and season with salt and pepper. Put the butter into the centre of each potato and top with the lentil mixture and goat's cheese slices. Bake uncovered for a further 15 minutes until the cheese is melted and golden on top.

5 Sprinkle over the remaining chopped parsley and serve immediately with a dollop of sour cream.

2 medium sized sweet potatoes, skin pierced in several places
100g (2 cups) cooked Puy lentils
1 small bunch of flat leaf parsley, finely chopped
1 tsp dried chipotle chilli flakes
1 tsp crushed coriander seeds
zest and juice of 1 lemon
olive oil
15g (1 tbsp) butter
75g (2½oz) goat's cheese, with rind, sliced
salt and freshly ground black pepper

To serve
sour cream

Serves 2

Suitable for

foil

parchment

oven bag

Stuffed peppers with mangetout salad

This takes a little bit of patience, as there is a lot of chopping involved, but you can do this while the aubergine is cooking in the oven. Once everything is prepared you can sit back, have a nice cold drink and wait for your dinner to cook itself.

1 Preheat the oven to 190°C fan (410°F/Gas 6–7). Line a baking dish with a large sheet of foil or parchment.

2 Tip the finely diced aubergine into the lined dish and spread into a thin layer. Drizzle with olive oil and season well. Carefully close up the parcel (you will need to open it up and close again so don't scrunch it too tightly) and bake for 25 minutes.

3 Meanwhile, prepare the filling. Mix the rice, corn, frozen peas, pine nuts, Parmesan and half of the chopped herbs together in a large bowl. Add about 1 tablespoon of olive oil and season well. Stir everything together and set aside.

4 Slice the tops off the peppers, about 1cm (½in) down, keeping the stalks on, and remove and discard the seeds. Set aside. Prepare 4 smaller sheets of parchment or foil.

5 Open up the parcel and tip the cooked aubergine into the bowl with the rice mixture and stir to combine. Fill each pepper, as full as you can, with this mixture and spread any remaining filling over the base of each of the 4 sheets of parchment or foil. Sit the peppers, with their hats on, on top. Drizzle everything with a little more olive oil and season again with salt and pepper. Close up the parcels and bake in the oven for 40 minutes.

6 Mix the remaining herbs with the mangetout, lemon juice and yogurt. Season with salt and pepper and set aside.

7 Remove the peppers from the oven and serve directly onto plates with the mangetout salad spooned over the top.

1 medium aubergine
  (eggplant), very finely diced
olive oil
100g (¾ cup) pre-cooked
  brown rice
100g (3½oz) baby corn,
  finely sliced
100g (⅔ cup) frozen peas
2 tbsp pine nuts
2 tbsp freshly grated Parmesan
8 sprigs of mint, leaves
  picked and finely chopped
5 sprigs of tarragon, leaves
  picked and finely chopped
a few sprigs of dill, stalks
  and leaves finely chopped
4 red Romano peppers
salt and freshly ground
  black pepper

For the mangetout salad
200g (7oz) mangetout (snow
  peas), finely sliced
a generous squeeze of
  lemon juice
3 tbsp Greek yogurt

Serves 4

Suitable for

foil

parchment

Fennel with plum tomatoes and Puy lentils

This is an adaptation from a recipe created by my favourite food writer, Diana Henry. Cooked tomatoes are, in my opinion, far superior to fresh ones and are on my desert-island list of foods. Here the fennel cooks so it is buttery soft in the middle and slightly chewy at the edges, and the lentils bring the whole dish together. This is best eaten warm or at room temperature and is a great summer supper.

1 Preheat the oven to 200°C fan (425°F/Gas 7). Line a baking dish with two large sheets of foil or parchment.

2 Put the fennel slices into a bowl with the garlic, orange zest and juice, fennel seeds, sumac and a generous glug of olive oil, and mix together. Season with salt and pepper and spread, in a single layer, in the lined baking dish.

3 Arrange the tomato halves on top, cut side up, and drizzle over the balsamic vinegar and a little more olive oil then season each tomato half with salt and pepper. Carefully close up the parcel, taking care to keep everything in a flat layer, and bake in the oven for 35 minutes.

4 Open up the parcel and return to the oven for another 20 minutes, until the fennel and tomatoes are caramelised. Scatter over the lentils and return to the oven for a final 10 minutes. You only want the lentils to warm through.

5 Roughly chop or pick the reserved fennel fronds and sprinkle these, together with the basil and parsley, over the hot lentils and veg.

6 Serve warm but not piping hot.

2 fennel bulbs, cut into 1-cm (½-in) slices, fronds reserved
2 garlic cloves, crushed or grated
zest and juice of 1 orange
1 tsp fennel seeds
1 tsp sumac
olive oil
6 plum tomatoes, halved
1 tbsp balsamic vinegar
1 x 250-g (9-oz) packet ready-cooked Puy lentils
1 small bunch of basil, roughly chopped or torn
1 small bunch of flat leaf parsley, roughly chopped
salt and freshly ground black pepper

Serves 4

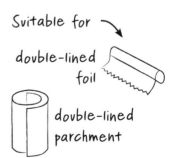

Suitable for

double-lined foil

double-lined parchment

Pasta e fagioli

This is a chunky vegetable and pasta stew and makes a perfect, healthy midweek meal. This is great with bacon, but if you want to keep this recipe meat-free leave it out and, instead, add the end of a block of Parmesan when you add the stock for extra umami flavour.

1 Preheat the oven to 180°C fan (400°F/Gas 6). Line a baking dish with two large sheets of foil, or an oven bag.

2 Mix the olive oil with the shallots, bacon (if using), courgette, leek, bay leaf and rosemary sprig in a bowl. Season generously with salt and pepper and tip into the lined baking dish. Bake, uncovered, in the oven for 30 minutes.

3 Remove from the oven, give everything a stir then add the beans, stock, chilli (if using), garlic, tomato purée, pasta, Parmesan (if using) and some salt and pepper and stir again. Carefully close up the bag or foil and return to the oven for 15 minutes. (If using an oven bag, snip a few slits in the top to allow steam to escape.)

4 Remove from the oven and serve in warmed shallow bowls with a drizzle of extra virgin olive oil, some basil and Parmesan.

2 tbsp olive oil
2 shallots, finely sliced
100g (3½oz) smoked bacon
   lardons (optional)
1 small courgette (zucchini),
   diced
1 small leek, thickly sliced
1 bay leaf
1 sprig of rosemary
1 x 400-g (14-oz) can borlotti
   beans, drained and rinsed
750ml (3¼cups) hot vegetable
   or chicken stock
1 red chilli, finely chopped
   (optional)
1 garlic clove, crushed
1 tbsp tomato purée (paste)
150g (5½oz) short pasta
end of a block of Parmesan
   (optional)
salt and freshly ground
   black pepper

To serve
extra virgin olive oil
fresh basil leaves
freshly grated Parmesan

Serves 4

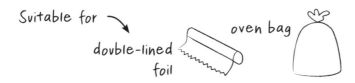
Suitable for → double-lined foil, oven bag

Mediterranean vegetables and halloumi with herb oil

This is an easy, unfussy dish you can serve to friends when you're too tired to cook. The garlic cloves are cooked in their skins – let people squeeze their own when serving rather than you doing it for them. You can throw in a can of drained chickpeas at the final stage of cooking if you want to bulk this dish up even more.

1 Preheat the oven to 200°C fan (425°F/Gas 7). Line a baking dish with two sheets of parchment or foil.

2 Pile the courgettes, onions, peppers, garlic cloves and olives into the lined baking dish and spread out in a thick-ish layer. Tuck in the oregano sprigs, drizzle over a good glug of olive oil and season generously with salt and pepper. Give everything a good mix and spread out again. Seal up the parcel (see pages 10–11), taking care to keep everything in an even layer, and bake for 30 minutes.

3 Remove from the oven, roll down the sides of the parchment, exposing all the vegetables, and add the halloumi slices in a single layer on top of the vegetables. Return to the oven, parchment open, for 20 minutes.

4 Meanwhile, make the herb oil. Finely chop the oregano leaves and basil and add to a bowl. Stir in the olive oil and season with salt and pepper. You may need more or less oil depending on the amounts of herbs you have. Ensure it's runnier than pesto so that you can drizzle it easily.

5 When the vegetables and halloumi have had their final cooking time, remove from the oven, and serve up with the herb oil drizzled over.

2 medium courgettes (zucchini), thickly sliced
2 red onions, cut into 1-cm (½-in) wedges
2 Romano peppers, tops and seeds removed, sliced into thick rings
10 garlic cloves, skins on
130g (generous 1 cup) pitted green olives
4 sprigs of fresh oregano
extra virgin olive oil
1 x 250-g (9-oz) block halloumi, sliced
salt and freshly ground black pepper

For the herb oil
1 small bunch of oregano, leaves only
1 small bunch of basil
approx. 50ml (1⅔fl oz) extra virgin olive oil
salt and freshly ground black pepper

Serves 4

Suitable for
double-lined foil
double-lined parchment

Leeks with Romesco sauce

This is a lovely starter for the summer or autumn and can be made a day ahead. It's ideal for al fresco dining and the sauce goes a long way so you could easily double the quantity of leeks to serve four – if you decide to do this then cook both batches of leeks in two separate parcels to keep the cooking time the same. Any leftover Romesco sauce is also delicious with white fish or chicken.

2 red (bell) peppers
1 medium sized ripe tomato
1 hot red chilli, left whole
2 large garlic cloves, skins on
100g (3½oz) blanched
   almonds
4 leeks
1 tbsp olive oil, plus extra
   for drizzling
2 tbsp red wine vinegar
¼ tsp hot smoked paprika
½ tsp sweet smoked paprika
salt and freshly ground
   black pepper

1 Preheat the oven to 200°C fan (425°F/Gas 7). Line two separate baking dishes with parchment or foil.

2 Halve the peppers, removing the seeds and stalks, and place, skin side up, in one of the lined baking dishes, along with the tomato, chilli, garlic and almonds. Seal up the parcel (see pages 10–11) and bake for 40 minutes, until the skin of the pepper is coming away and the flesh is soft.

3 Wash the leeks and slice in half lengthways. Lay on the second lined baking dish in a single layer, drizzle with the tablespoon of olive oil and season generously with salt and pepper. Seal up and bake for 30 minutes.

4 When the pepper is cool enough to handle, remove the skin. Squeeze the garlic cloves out of their skins and roughly chop the tomato and the chilli. Blend the pepper, garlic, tomato, chilli and almonds together in a food processor with the red wine vinegar, both smoked paprikas and a drizzle of olive oil to loosen. Season with salt and pepper.

5 Serve the leeks either warm or at room temperature with the sauce poured over and a sprinkling of toasted flaked almonds.

To serve
flaked (slivered) almonds,
   toasted

Serves 2

Suitable for

foil

parchment

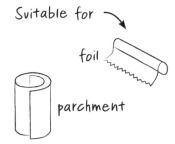

Baby vegetables with orange and thyme

This is a great side dish and would go well with the Roast chicken with fennel on page 93 or as an accompaniment to the Whole baked salmon on page 67. The vegetables steam and come out on the firmer side of *al dente* so if you prefer yours cooked a little more, add on 10 minutes to the overall cooking time.

1 Preheat the oven to 200°C fan (425°F/Gas 7). Line a baking dish with parchment or foil, or an oven bag.

2 Mix the carrots and courgettes with the orange zest, juice, olive oil and lots of salt and pepper in a bowl.

3 Pile into the lined baking dish, drizzling over any juice that gets left behind in the bowl. Add the thyme sprigs then close up the parcel (see pages 10–11) and bake for 45–55 minutes. (If using an oven bag, snip a few slits in the top to allow steam to escape.)

300g (10½oz) baby carrots, scrubbed and green tops removed
400g (7oz) baby courgettes (zucchini), halved lengthways
zest and juice of 1 large orange
2 tbsp olive oil
a few sprigs of lemon thyme

Serves 3–4

Suitable for

foil

parchment

oven bag

FISH

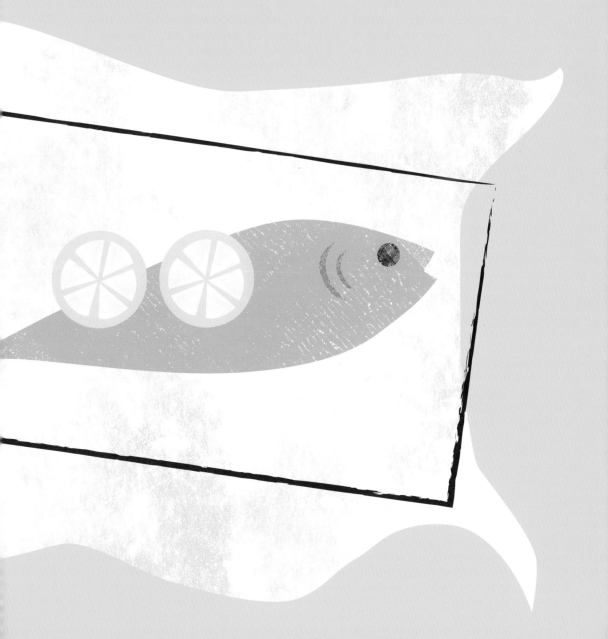

Cod en papillote with spinach, olives and Mediterranean herbs

This looks beautiful and is very good for you – all that spinach! You can happily double this recipe to serve four but I'd recommend you cook it in two separate parcels to ensure the fish cooks evenly.

1 Preheat the oven to 200°C fan (425°F/Gas 7). Line a baking dish with a large piece of parchment or foil, or an oven bag.

2 Finely chop the olives, anchovy fillets and herbs together. Mix together with juice from half of the lemon in a bowl, season with salt and pepper and add a little glug of olive oil.

3 In a separate bowl, combine the butter beans with the spinach leaves and two-thirds of the olive and herb mixture. Drizzle in a little more olive oil and season well with salt and pepper. Tip into the lined baking dish and spread everything out evenly.

4 Slice the remaining lemon half into 4–6 slices and lay these on top of the spinach and beans. Place the cod loins on top of the lemon slices, season with salt and pepper and spread the remaining herby olive mixture over the fish. Close up the parcel (see pages 10–11) and bake in the oven for 15–20 minutes. (If using an oven bag, snip a few slits in the top to allow steam to escape.)

5 When cooked, unwrap and serve with the radish slices and pea shoots scattered over the top.

60g (generous ½ cup) pitted black olives
2 anchovy fillets in oil
4 thyme stalks, leaves picked
4 oregano stalks, leaves picked
1 small bunch of flat leaf parsley
1 lemon
olive oil
1 x 400-g (14-oz) can butter beans, drained and rinsed
120g (4¼oz) baby leaf spinach, washed
2 cod loins (approx. 150g/ 5½oz each)
salt and freshly ground black pepper

To serve
6 radishes, sliced
a handful of pea shoots

Serves 2

Suitable for

foil

parchment

oven bag

Seabream with broccoli, new potatoes and lemon rocket sauce

This is an easy but delicious one-pot recipe which has all you need to feed four. Beautiful seabream glimmers alongside some simply cooked potatoes and broccoli.

1 Preheat the oven to 200°C fan (425°F/Gas 7). Line a baking dish with a large piece of parchment or foil.

2 Scatter the halved potatoes into the lined baking dish. (You will eventually add the broccoli and the fish on top so make sure they will fit in a layer on top of the potatoes.) Drizzle the potatoes with 1 tablespoon of the olive oil and season well with salt and pepper. Close up the parcel and bake in the oven for 50 minutes.

3 Meanwhile, make the sauce. Put the rocket, remaining olive oil, lemon zest and juice and Parmesan into a large bowl and blend with a stick blender until you have a thick-ish sauce. You can use a small food blender or pestle and mortar if you prefer. Season with salt and pepper and set aside.

4 Dry the skin of the seabream with kitchen paper and season the fish well on both sides.

5 After 50 minutes, open up the potato parcel and scatter over the broccoli. Reseal the parcel and bake for another 10 minutes. If you prefer your broccoli less *al dente*, cook for 15 minutes.

6 Open up the parcel a final time, add the seabream (skin side up and spaced well apart) and drizzle the skin with a little olive oil. Roast, uncovered, for 8 minutes. The fish is cooked when the flesh is opaque all the way through.

7 Divide the potatoes, broccoli and fish between four warmed plates and drizzle over the lemon rocket sauce.

800g (1lb 12oz) Jersey Royal potatoes, halved
3 tbsp extra virgin olive oil, plus extra for drizzling
60g (2¼oz) rocket (arugula), washed
zest of 1 lemon, juice of ½
1 tbsp freshly grated Parmesan
4 x 120–150-g (4¼–5½-oz) seabream fillets
250g (9oz) Tenderstem broccoli, trimmed, large pieces halved
salt and freshly ground black pepper

Serves 4

Suitable for

foil

parchment

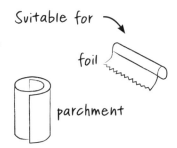

Haddock with Asian spices and brown rice

Cooking with pre-cooked rice really does slash the cooking time, with this recipe taking no more than 30 minutes – ideal for a midweek dinner.

1 Preheat the oven to 180°C fan (400°F/Gas 6). Line a baking dish with parchment or foil, or an oven bag.

2 Tip the brown rice into the lined baking dish. Season the haddock fillets generously with salt and pepper and place both fillets on top of the rice. Add the star anise, ginger, chilli, garlic, soy sauce and sunflower oil. Close the parcel (see pages 10–11) and bake in the oven for 10 minutes. (If using an oven bag, snip a few slits in the top to allow steam to escape.)

3 Remove from the oven and carefully open up the parcel; add the pak choi leaves, seal the parcel again and return to the oven for 5 minutes.

4 Remove from the oven and allow to stand for 5 minutes before carefully opening the parcel. Divide the fish, greens and rice between two plates, taking care to scrape over all the juices.

1 x 250-g (9-oz) packet
   pre-cooked brown rice
2 x skinless haddock fillets
   (approx. 300g/10½oz
   total weight)
2 whole star anise
2-cm (¾-in) piece of fresh
   ginger, julienned
1 hot chilli, finely sliced
1 garlic clove, finely sliced
1 tbsp light soy sauce
½ tbsp sunflower oil
2 heads pak choi,
   leaves separated
salt and freshly ground
   black pepper

Serves 2

Suitable for

foil

parchment

oven bag /
Stasher bag

Tuna with pickled red onions, tomatoes and salsa verde

This is a lovely light supper which takes only 30 minutes from start to finish. The tuna can be flaked at the end or left whole, depending on how you like to serve it. The salsa verde makes more than you need but keeps for a week or so in the fridge and is great with almost any fish, lamb or chicken.

1 Preheat the oven to 190°C fan (410°F/Gas 6–7). Prepare two large squares of parchment or foil separately on a baking dish. (Alternatively, line a baking dish with an oven bag.)

2 Mix the red onion with the vinegar, salt and sugar in a small bowl and set aside while you prepare the rest of the dish.

3 Divide the cherry tomatoes between the two squares. Add the chickpeas, season with salt and pepper and drizzle over the olive oil. Sit a tuna steak on top of each, season and squeeze over the lemon juice. Close up the parcels (see pages 10–11) and bake in the oven for 25 minutes. (If using an oven bag, snip a few slits in the top to allow steam to escape.)

4 Meanwhile, make the salsa verde. Put the parsley, dill, mint, capers, lemon juice and olive oil in a pestle and mortar and crush together. Alternatively, use a small food blender.

5 Remove the parcels from the oven, open up them up and gently squash some of the tomatoes to release their juices. Serve directly onto warmed plates and scatter with the salsa verde and pickled red onions.

½ red onion, thinly sliced
1 tbsp apple cider vinegar
1 tsp salt
½ tbsp caster (superfine) sugar
250g (9oz) cherry tomatoes on the vine, snipped into small bunches
1 x 400-g (14-oz) can chickpeas (garbanzos), drained and rinsed
½ tbsp olive oil
2 x 120-g (4¼-oz) yellowfin tuna steaks
juice of ½ lemon
salt and freshly ground black pepper

For the salsa verde
4 parsley stalks with leaves, roughly chopped
4 dill stalks with leaves, roughly chopped
4 mint stalks, leaves picked and roughly chopped
½ tbsp small (non-pareil) capers, rinsed
juice of ½ lemon
½ tbsp olive oil

Serves 2

Suitable for

foil

parchment

oven bag

Mussels with fennel and Pernod

Glossy mussels with three types of aniseed – yummy! This is an alternative method to cooking mussels in a pot on the stove and you won't have any washing up to do. Best cooked in an oven bag, to keep the steam in, but it also cooks well in double-lined parchment or foil.

1 Preheat the oven to 200°C fan (425°F/Gas 7). Line a baking dish with two sheets of parchment or foil, or an oven bag.

2 Soak the mussels in a bowl of cold water for 10 minutes. Remove any beards, scrape off the barnacles and discard any with cracked or open shells.

3 Mix the celery, shallot, chopped fennel and seeds with the olive oil and a good pinch of salt and pepper in a large bowl. Spoon into the lined baking dish and bake in the oven for 20 minutes – don't close up the parcel yet as you want the veggies to get a little colour on them.

4 Pour over the Pernod and bake in the same way for a further 4 minutes. Add the mussels, close up the parcel (see pages 10–11) and bake for another 15 minutes, until all the mussels have opened. (If using an oven bag, snip a few slits in the top to allow steam to escape.)

5 Remove from the oven, open up the parcel, discard any mussels that haven't opened, then add the double cream, basil and reserved fennel fronds and mix everything together. Serve with big chunks of buttered bread to mop up the juices.

1kg (2lb 4oz) fresh mussels
1 stick celery, finely sliced
1 banana shallot, finely chopped
1 fennel bulb, finely chopped, fronds reserved for garnish
1 tsp fennel seeds
1 tbsp olive oil
60ml (¼ cup) Pernod
100ml (generous ⅓ cup) double (heavy) cream
a few basil leaves, roughly chopped or torn
salt and freshly ground black pepper

To serve
plenty of crusty bread

Serves 2

Suitable for

double-lined foil

double-lined parchment

oven bag

Salmon with lemon, asparagus, potatoes and garlic butter

This is a healthy, vibrant all-in-one dish, worthy of serving to friends and family. Try to use Pink Fir Apple or Anya potatoes if you can get hold of them – but the more common Charlotte potato is great too. Make as a lovely early summer dish when asparagus is in season and at its best.

1 Preheat the oven to 200°C fan (425°F/Gas 7). Line a large baking dish with a large sheet of foil or parchment.

2 Place the salmon fillets on a plate, season with salt and pepper, sprinkle over the lemon zest and set aside.

3 In a large bowl, mix the potatoes with the spring onions, 2 tablespoons of the olive oil and the lemon juice then season with salt and pepper. Tip the potatoes and spring onions onto the foil or parchment and seal the parcel (see pages 10–11). Bake in the oven for 40 minutes.

4 The potatoes should now be almost tender. Carefully unfold the parcel and tuck in the asparagus and cherry tomatoes. Place the salmon fillets, skin side up, on top, drizzle with the remaining olive oil and cook, with the parcel open, for a further 10–15 minutes, until just cooked through.

5 Meanwhile mix the melted butter, crushed garlic and chopped dill together in a bowl.

6 Serve the salmon and vegetables straight away with the garlic butter brushed over the top of the fish.

4 x 150-g salmon fillets, skin on
zest and juice of ½ lemon
750g (1lb 10oz) new potatoes, large ones halved or quartered
1 bunch of spring onions (scallions), sliced
3 tbsp olive oil
1 bunch of asparagus, trimmed and halved lengthways
150g (5½oz) cherry tomatoes
salt and freshly ground black pepper

For the garlic butter
75g (⅓ cup) salted butter, melted
1 garlic clove, crushed
1 small bunch of dill, chopped

Serves 4

Suitable for

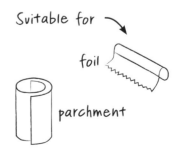

foil

parchment

Italian salmon packets with couscous

This delicious dish takes almost no time at all and the Italian flavours of black olives and cherry tomatoes taste heavenly with the oily salmon.

1 Preheat the oven to 180°C fan (400°F/Gas 6). Line a baking dish with parchment or foil, or an oven bag.

2 Season the salmon fillets and set aside on a plate.

3 Mix half of the oregano and basil with all of the olives and 1 tablespoon of the olive oil in a bowl and season with salt and pepper. Smear over the flesh side of the salmon fillets, then place the fillets into the lined baking dish, alternating with slices of red onion and cherry tomatoes until the bag is full. Seal up the parcel (see pages 10–11) and bake for 20–25 minutes. (If using an oven bag, snip a few slits in the top to allow steam to escape.)

4 Put the couscous into a wide heatproof bowl and season with salt and pepper. Pour over the hot stock and the remaining olive oil, cover with cling film and set aside for 10 minutes. Fluff up with a fork and stir in the remaining chopped herbs just before serving.

5 Serve the salmon and vegetables on top of the couscous with lemon wedges on the side.

4 x 150-g (5½-oz) salmon fillets, skin on
5 oregano stalks, leaves picked and chopped
1 small bunch of basil, finely chopped
70g (generous ½ cup) pitted black olives, finely chopped
2 tbsp extra virgin olive oil
½ red onion, very finely sliced
240g (9oz) cherry tomatoes on the vine, snipped into bunches
240g (scant 1½ cups) uncooked couscous
360ml (1½ cups) hot vegetable stock
salt and freshly ground black pepper

To serve
1 lemon, cut into wedges

Serves 4

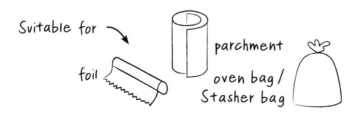

Suitable for

foil

parchment

oven bag / Stasher bag

56

Lemon sole with potatoes, capers, lemon and herbs

Lemon sole is so delicate and barely needs any cooking. It's super-easy to prepare but will feel luxurious to whoever you are feeding, so keep the simplicity a secret! Serve this with a green salad or some steamed green veg.

1 Preheat the oven to 200°C fan (425°F/Gas 7). Line a baking dish with parchment or foil.

2 Drizzle the potato slices with half of the olive oil and season well with salt and pepper, then arrange them in a single layer in the lined baking dish. Seal up the parcel (see pages 10–11) and bake for 30 minutes.

3 While the potatoes are cooking, make the marinade for the fish. Mix the remaining olive oil with the capers, lemon zest and juice, dill, parsley and mustard in a bowl and season well. Slice the sole fillets in half horizontally to create four pieces of fish, then season on both sides with salt and pepper. Lay the sole on a large plate and spread the marinade over the flesh side of each piece of fish. Set aside, until the potatoes are ready.

4 Once the potatoes have had 30 minutes, open up the parcel and lay the fish fillets on top, marinade side down. Smear a little butter on each fillet, then bake in the oven, uncovered, for 10 minutes. Remove from the oven and serve immediately.

500g (1lb 2oz) Charlotte or Anya potatoes, washed and cut into 1-cm (½-in) slices
2 tbsp olive oil
1 tbsp small (non-pareil) capers, rinsed and roughly chopped
zest of 1 lemon, juice of ½
1 tbsp chopped dill
1 tbsp chopped flat leaf parsley
½ tbsp Dijon mustard
4 medium (approx. 130g/4½oz) lemon sole fillets, skin on
10g (⅓oz) butter
salt and freshly ground black pepper

Serves 4

Suitable for

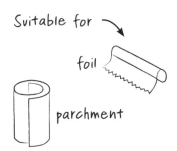

foil

parchment

Halibut with creamy vegetables and potatoes

Halibut is a lovely meaty fish which takes on flavour well. This dish is a good one-pot meal that could be doubled up to feed four. Use a waxy potato like Charlotte or Anya as they will hold their shape well.

1 Preheat the oven to 190°C fan (410°F/Gas 6–7). Line a baking dish with parchment or foil, or an oven bag.

2 Put the potatoes, bacon lardons (if using) and leeks into the lined baking dish, drizzle with a little olive oil and season with lots of salt and pepper. Keep the parcel open and bake for 50 minutes, stirring halfway through. The potatoes should be just tender.

3 Place the halibut fillets on a plate, season with salt and pepper and sprinkle over the lemon zest and set aside.

4 Once the potatoes, leeks and bacon (if using) have had 50 minutes, pour in the double cream and add the peas and lemon juice. Season everything again and mix together. Arrange the halibut fillets on top, close up the parcel (see pages 10–11) and bake for a further 10–12 minutes, until the fish is cooked through. (If using an oven bag, snip a few slits in the top to allow steam to escape.)

5 Remove from the oven and serve immediately.

400g (14oz) waxy new potatoes, halved
50g (1¾oz) smoked bacon lardons (optional)
2 small leeks, thickly sliced
olive oil
2 x 150-g (5½-oz) thick halibut fillets
zest and juice of ½ lemon
150ml (⅔ cup) double (heavy) cream
150g (1 cup) frozen peas
salt and freshly ground black pepper

Serves 2 generously

Suitable for

foil
parchment
oven bag

Seafood pasta

This is a classic dish cooked *en papillotte*. I've made it here in four separate parcels, so each person gets to unwrap their own parcel on a plate, but you can also cook everything together in an oven bag. The flavours are delicate with lots of fishiness coming from the mussels and prawn shells. You can add some chopped red chilli to the parcels before they go in the oven if you want a little kick.

1 Preheat the oven to 200°C fan (425°F/Gas 7). Prepare four large squares of parchment or foil on two baking dishes. (Alternatively, line a baking dish with an oven bag.)

2 In a large bowl, cover the pasta with boiling water and set aside while you prepare the shellfish.

3 Soak the mussels in a bowl of cold water for 10 minutes. Remove any beards, scrape off the barnacles and discard any with cracked or open shells. Cut the scallops in half and separate the coral roe. Cut the squid into ½-cm (¼-in) rings.

4 Brush the four squares of parchment or foil with half of the melted butter. Drain the pasta and distribute it evenly between the parcel squares. Top with the mussels, scallops and roe, squid rings and prawns. Season each pile of pasta and shellfish generously with salt and pepper and scatter over the herbs. Pour over the white wine, taking care none escapes out of the sides, and drizzle over the remaining melted butter. Close each parcel tightly (see pages 10–11). (If using an oven bag, snip a few slits in the top to allow steam to escape.)

5 Bake the parcels, set well apart, in the oven for 20 minutes, until the mussels have opened, the prawns are pink and the scallops are cooked.

6 Allow to stand for a couple of minutes before serving each parcel directly onto warmed plates. Squeeze over a generous amount of lemon juice and eat immediately.

400g (14oz) fresh tagliatelle
600g (1lb 5oz) fresh mussels
4 large scallops
4 baby squid (about 100g/3½oz), cleaned, quills and beaks removed
100g (3½oz) butter, melted, plus extra for brushing
150g (5½oz) raw king prawns, (jumbo shrimp) shells and heads left on
1 small bunch of flat leaf parsley, finely chopped
½ small bunch of fennel herb or dill, finely chopped
150ml (⅔ cup) dry white wine
salt and freshly ground black pepper

To serve
lemon wedges

Serves 4

Suitable for

foil

parchment

oven bag

King prawns with paprika and cherry tomatoes

This is a starter-sized dish a bit like the Spanish dish *gambas al ajillo* but here I've added in chorizo and cherry tomatoes for even more flavour. You could easily omit the chorizo if you want to keep this dish pescatarian. Be sure to serve with a good loaf of crusty bread to mop up the garlicky oil.

1 Preheat the oven to 200°C fan (425°F/Gas 7). Line a baking dish with parchment or foil, or an oven bag.

2 Remove the tails and body shells from the prawns but keep the heads on for added flavour. In a bowl, mix the prawns with the chorizo (if using), garlic, paprika, tomatoes and olive oil. Season generously with salt and pepper then tip into the lined baking dish. Close up the parcel (see pages 10–11) and bake in the oven for 30 minutes. (If using an oven bag, snip a few slits in the top to allow steam to escape.)

3 Remove from the oven and check all the prawns are pink and there is no grey at all. If there is, return to the oven for another 5 minutes, uncovered.

4 Allow to sit for a few minutes before serving with lots of crusty bread.

400g (14oz) fresh king prawns (jumbo shrimp), shells and heads left on
120g (4¼oz) cooking chorizo, finely diced (optional)
3 large garlic cloves, finely sliced
1 tsp hot smoked paprika
250g (9oz) yellow and red cherry tomatoes on the vine, snipped into smaller bunches
150ml (⅔ cup) extra virgin olive oil
salt and freshly ground black pepper

To serve
plenty of crusty bread

Serves 2 as a starter or light lunch

Suitable for

foil

parchment

oven bag / Stasher bag

Baked side of salmon with a herb crust

If you have many mouths to feed and want to produce an impressive dish, this is the recipe for you. The bright-green crust contrasts beautifully with the pink salmon. Wild garlic is best during the spring months so if you want to make this at other times of the year you could swap in the same weight of basil and add 4 crushed garlic cloves.

1 Preheat the oven to 200°C fan (425°F/Gas 7). Line a baking dish with parchment or foil (big enough to wrap around the whole fish).

2 Pat the salmon dry with kitchen paper and lay, skin side down, in the lined baking dish. Season the fish with salt and pepper.

3 Place the lemon zest, wild garlic, oregano leaves, thyme, Parmesan and breadcrumbs in a food processor and blitz until finely chopped. Spread the topping evenly over the surface of the salmon in a thick layer.

4 Loosely fold up the parcel, taking care not to press onto the crust itself, and bake in the oven for 10 minutes. Open up the parcel fully and place back in the oven for a further 10–15 minutes for the crust to brown and the fish to finish cooking.

5 Remove from the oven and allow to stand for a few minutes before serving with wedges of lemon.

1 side of salmon, approx. 850g–1kg (1lb 14oz–2lb 4oz), skin on
zest of 1 lemon
a handful of wild garlic leaves, about 50g (1¾oz)
4 stalks of oregano, leaves picked
1 tbsp thyme leaves
3 heaped tbsp freshly grated Parmesan
5 tbsp fresh breadcrumbs
salt and freshly ground black pepper

To serve
lemon wedges (from the zested lemon)

Serves 6–8, depending on the size of the salmon

Suitable for

foil

parchment

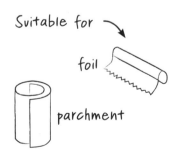

Haddock gratin with broccoli

This is a super-easy, one-pot fish gratin perfect for winter months. It's light on carbs so if you're feeling very hungry you may want to cook some potatoes to serve on the side. I am a heathen and will always have tomato ketchup with creamy fish pies, especially if it's winter, so I've seized the opportunity to suggest it here. If you don't want to use ready-made bechamel, swap in the same quantity of crème fraîche.

1 Preheat the oven to 200°C fan (425°F/Gas 7). Line a small, deep baking dish with parchment or foil.

2 Combine the haddock strips with the bechamel, cream and lemon juice in a bowl. Add 60g (2oz) of the Gruyère and half of the chopped parsley and basil, then season generously with salt and pepper and mix together. Tip into the lined baking dish, distribute the broccoli evenly amongst the fish then close up the parcel (see pages 10–11). Bake in the oven for 20 minutes.

3 Meanwhile, make the gratin topping. Mix the remaining Gruyère and herbs with the breadcrumbs and set aside.

4 Remove the fish from the oven, open up the parcel and sprinkle over the gratin topping. Dot the butter over the top and return to the oven, uncovered, for 20 minutes, until the breadcrumbs are golden and crispy and the cheese has melted.

5 Put on your pyjamas, cosy up and serve the gratin with some ketchup on the side.

450g (1lb) haddock fillets, skin off, cut into 1-cm (½-in) strips
250g (9oz) ready-made or leftover bechamel sauce
200ml (generous ⅔ cup) double (heavy) cream
juice of 1 lemon
100g (3½oz) Gruyère cheese, grated
1 small bunch of flat leaf parsley, finely chopped
1 small bunch of basil, finely chopped
½ head broccoli, cut into small florets
40g (1½oz) fresh breadcrumbs
15g (1 tbsp) butter
salt and freshly ground black pepper

To serve
tomato ketchup (optional)

Serves 2 generously

Suitable for

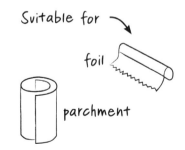

foil

parchment

Mussels with lemongrass, chilli, ginger and lime

I was taught this dish when I lived with a fabulous family in Pitlochry back in 2002. I had just left university and got a job working with them for a few months, and it was one of the happiest times for me. We foraged for chanterelles, poured wine into a crock to make vinegar, used up produce from the kitchen garden and made yogurt daily. Whenever we had lots of guests this soupy dish would always be served to exclamations of delight.

1 Preheat the oven to 200°C fan (425°F/Gas 7). Line a baking dish with two sheets of parchment, one sheet of foil, or an oven bag.

2 Soak the mussels in a bowl of cold water for 10 minutes. Remove any beards, scrape off the barnacles and discard any with cracked or open shells. In another bowl, cover the noodles with boiling water and set aside.

3 Drain the mussels and spread out in the lined baking tray along with the lemongrass, chilli and ginger. Carefully pour over the wine then close up the parcel. Bake in the oven for 15 minutes. (If using an oven bag, snip a few slits in the top to allow steam to escape.)

4 Meanwhile, in a large serving bowl, whisk together the lime zest, juice, sugar, peanut oil, chilli flakes, red onion, coriander and some salt and pepper. Drain the noodles and drop them in, stirring briefly to coat them in the dressing.

5 Remove the mussels from the oven and allow to stand for a few minutes. Open up the parcel and discard any which have not fully opened. Prise two thirds of the mussels from their shells and drop into the serving bowl with the noodles. Discard the empty shells then pour the remaining contents of the parcel into the large serving bowl and mix carefully, making sure everything is covered in the dressing. Serve immediately.

1kg (2lb 4oz) fresh mussels
500g (1lb 2oz) cooked egg
   noodles
2 lemongrass sticks, finely sliced
2 bird's eye chillies, lightly
   bashed but left whole
5-cm (2-in) piece of fresh
   ginger, finely grated
200ml (scant ¾ cup) dry
   white wine
zest and juice of 2 limes
1½ tsp soft dark brown sugar
100ml (generous ⅓ cup)
   peanut oil
1 tsp dried chilli flakes
½ red onion, finely chopped
1 bunch of coriander (cilantro),
   finely chopped
salt and freshly ground
   black pepper

Serves 2 generously

Suitable for

foil

parchment

oven bag

Whole baked mackerel with tomato and avocado salad

Mackerel is one of the best oily fish you can eat, in my opinion. It is inexpensive and plentiful in the autumn and winter months when they are no longer spawning. This recipe calls for whole fish so ask your fishmonger to gut them for you.

1 Preheat the oven to 200°C fan (425°F/Gas 7). Prepare four large sheets of parchment or foil – one for each fish.

2 Mix the tomatoes, avocado, 2 tablespoons of the olive oil, salt and pepper and half of the basil leaves together in a bowl and set aside.

3 In another bowl, mix the cannellini beans with the crushed garlic then spoon them evenly between each piece of parchment or foil. Drizzle over a little olive oil and season with salt and pepper. Lay the mackerel on top of each pile of beans, tuck in the remaining basil leaves around each fish and season again with salt and pepper. Close up each parcel (see pages 10–11) and transfer to a baking dish. Bake for 20–25 minutes until the fish is fully cooked. The skin will peel away easily and the flesh will be opaque.

4 Meanwhile, mix the crème fraîche with the horseradish and season with salt and pepper.

5 Remove the fish and bean parcels from the oven and serve directly onto plates. Spoon over the tomato and avocado salad, scatter with watercress and dollop over some horseradish crème fraîche. Squeeze over some lemon juice and tuck in.

300g (10½oz) heritage
 tomatoes, sliced
2 avocados, sliced
3 tbsp olive oil, plus extra
 for drizzling
a small handful of basil leaves
2 x 400-g (14-oz) can of
 cannellini beans, drained
 and rinsed
1 garlic clove, crushed
4 whole fresh mackerel,
 gutted and cleaned
salt and freshly ground
 black pepper

For the horseradish cream
4 tbsp crème fraîche
4 tsp fresh horseradish (from
 approx. 4-cm/1½-in stick,
 finely grated)

To serve
120g (4¼oz) watercress
lemon wedges

Serves 4

Suitable for

foil

parchment

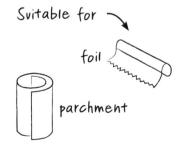

MEAT

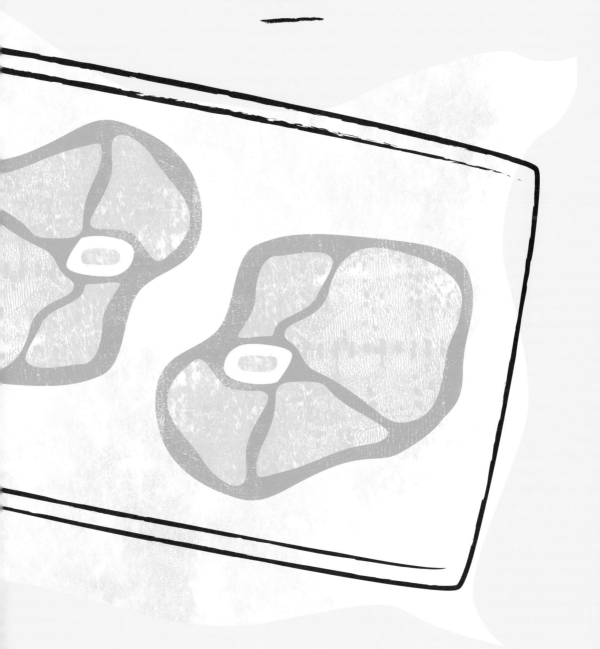

Chicken with prosciutto and thyme

This is a classic dish and great for entertaining, as you can prepare it the day before, wrap it up in foil, then pop it straight into the oven an hour before you want to eat.

1 Preheat the oven to 180°C fan (400°F/Gas 6). Prepare four sheets of foil or parchment, or oven bags, large enough to wrap up each chicken breast.

2 Butterfly the chicken breasts by cutting through the side of each breast towards the other side (but not all the way through) and opening it up like a book. Season each breast with salt and pepper, then spread half a tablespoon of the pesto over the inside of each one. Add some mozzarella to one side then fold the other side back over the top to make a whole chicken breast again.

3 Wrap 2 slices of prosciutto around each chicken breast and tuck the ends underneath. Carefully transfer them onto the sheets of foil or parchment, or into oven bags, then drizzle each with olive oil and season again with salt and pepper. Tuck a few artichoke halves around each breast and add a bunch of cherry tomatoes to each parcel. Add a couple of thyme sprigs to each then carefully seal up the parcels (see pages 10–11), leaving some space for the air to circulate inside them. (If using an oven bag, snip a few slits in the top to allow steam to escape.) At this point you can pop them in the fridge if cooking the next day.

4 Place the parcels, spaced well apart, in one or two baking dishes and bake for 30 minutes (40 minutes if cooking from chilled), then open up the foil parcels and return to the oven for 10 minutes to crisp up the prosciutto. To check the chicken is cooked, pierce with a skewer and any juices should run clear.

5 Scatter the chopped basil on top and serve with some boiled new potatoes and greens, if you like.

4 skinless, boneless chicken breasts
2 tbsp basil pesto
1 ball of mozzarella, torn into strips
8 slices of prosciutto
olive oil
8 canned grilled artichoke hearts, halved
250g (9oz) cherry tomatoes on the vine, snipped into 4 bunches
8 sprigs of thyme
1 small bunch of basil, roughly chopped
salt and freshly ground black pepper

Serves 4

Suitable for
foil
parchment
oven bag

Ginger, lime and chilli chicken with brown rice

Cooking chicken breasts in this way means they don't dry out and are deliciously tender. If you like things spicy then add a finely chopped bird's eye chilli to the rice. All the juices soak down into the rice, so make sure you scrape them up from the bottom of the parcel when you are dishing up.

1 Preheat the oven to 190°C fan (410°F/Gas 6–7). Line a baking dish with parchment or foil, or an oven bag.

2 Spread the rice over the lined baking dish and arrange the ginger slices, whole chilli and lime slices on top.

3 Season the chicken breasts with salt and pepper and place on top of the rice and aromatics. Sprinkle over half of the coriander and pour over the vegetable oil and soy sauce. Tuck the baby corn in around the sides of the chicken then fold the parcel to seal tightly (see pages 10–11). (If using an oven bag, snip a few slits in the top to allow steam to escape.)

4 Bake in the oven for 45 minutes. Check the chicken is cooked (pierce with a skewer and any juices should run clear), returning it to the oven for another 10 minutes if it's not quite there, then remove and leave to rest for 5 minutes.

5 Mix the remaining coriander with the yogurt and crushed coriander seeds in a small bowl and season with salt and pepper. Serve the chicken and rice with the coriander yogurt and a squeeze of fresh lime.

1 x 250-g (9-oz) packet
    pre-cooked brown rice
2-cm (¾-in) piece of fresh
    ginger, peeled and sliced
1 hot red chilli, left whole
    and bashed
1 lime, sliced
2 skinless, boneless chicken
    breasts
1 small bunch of coriander
    (cilantro), roughly chopped
1 tbsp vegetable oil
1 tbsp light soy sauce
175g (6oz) baby corn
100g (½ cup) Greek yogurt
1 tsp coriander seeds,
    crushed
salt and freshly ground
    black pepper

To serve
lime wedges

Serves 2

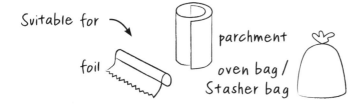
Suitable for

foil   parchment   oven bag / Stasher bag

Pork with ginger, coconut rice and salad

I'm a big fan of ready-made coconut rice – I can't get enough of it – and juicy pork fillet is both economical and quick to cook, so this is great for a quick and filling weekday dinner.

1 Preheat the oven to 180°C fan (400°F/Gas 6). Line a baking dish with parchment or foil, or an oven bag.

2 Mix the soy sauce, honey, grated ginger and sesame oil together in a bowl. Add the pork fillet pieces and mix together.

3 Tip the rice out into the middle of the lined baking dish. Arrange the pork pieces on top and pour over the marinade. Close up the parcel (see pages 10–11) and bake in the oven for 25–30 minutes (If using an oven bag, snip a few slits in the top to allow steam to escape), or until the pork is thoroughly cooked through (there should be no pink meat).

4 While the pork and rice are cooking, combine all the ingredients for the salad in a bowl squeezing over the lime juice and adding the olive oil. Season well with salt and pepper, toss the salad together and set aside.

5 When the pork is cooked, open up the parcel and scatter over the cashews.

6 Serve immediately with the salad on the side.

1 tbsp light soy sauce
1 tbsp runny honey
2-cm (¾-in) piece of fresh ginger, grated
½ tbsp toasted sesame oil
300g (10½oz) pork fillet, cut into 2-cm (¾-in) chunks, fat and sinew removed
1 x 250-g (9-oz) packet pre-cooked coconut rice
50g (⅓ cup) cashews, toasted and roughly chopped

For the salad

2 spring onions (scallions), sliced
1 bunch of coriander (cilantro), roughly chopped
1 bunch of mint, leaves picked and roughly chopped
1 hot chilli, deseeded and finely sliced
½ large cucumber, halved lengthways, deseeded and thinly sliced
100g (3½oz) cherry tomatoes, quartered
juice of 1 lime
1½ tbsp olive oil
salt and freshly ground black pepper

Serves 2

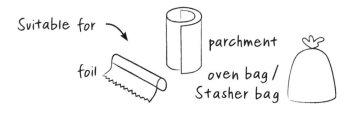

Suitable for

foil

parchment

oven bag / Stasher bag

Veggie | Fish | **Meat** | Desserts

Korean barbecue ribs with spring onions and sesame seeds

This is messy but great for sharing – my kind of food. The ribs will need basting during the last 30 minutes of cooking to prevent them from drying out, so don't miss out this step. You can finish these off on a barbecue if you like, but reserve some sauce so you can baste them regularly, as they will burn easily.

1 Preheat the oven to 180°C fan (400°F/Gas 6). Line a baking dish with parchment or foil. You might need to join two sheets together to ensure the ribs can be covered in one layer.

2 Season the pork ribs generously with salt and pepper and sit them in the lined dish. Fold up the parcel around the ribs (see pages 10–11) and bake in the oven for 1½ hours.

3 Meanwhile, in a small bowl, stir the onion, garlic, ginger, honey, sugar, soy sauce, sesame oil, vinegar, water and sesame seeds together. Set aside.

4 After 1½ hours, increase the oven temperature to 200°C (425°F/Gas 7) and remove the ribs from the oven. Carefully open up the parcel and pour the sauce ingredients over the ribs, ensuring the pork is well covered. Return to the oven, uncovered, for another 30 minutes, turning the ribs and basting halfway through. The sauce should be dark and sticky. Don't worry if the edges catch during cooking; this is completely normal!

5 Cut the ribs into pieces and serve with some sesame seeds and the spring onions sprinkled over the top. To make into a more substantial meal, serve with some fluffy white rice and steamed Asian greens.

1kg (2lb 4oz) pork loin rib racks
½ medium onion, grated
3 garlic cloves, grated or
   crushed
2.5-cm (1-in) piece of fresh
   ginger, grated
2 tbsp runny honey
40g (¼ cup) soft dark
   brown sugar
80ml (⅓ cup) light soy sauce
2 tsp toasted sesame oil
2 tbsp rice (or white/cider)
   vinegar
50ml (3 tbsp) water
1 tbsp sesame seeds, plus
   extra to serve
salt and freshly ground
   black pepper

To serve
4 spring onions (scallions),
   finely sliced

Serves 3–4

Suitable for

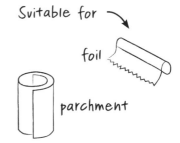

foil

parchment

Oriental beef with shiitake mushrooms

This is a great recipe that you can chuck in the oven and leave for a couple of hours while you do something else, safe in the knowledge that your dinner is on its way. It is rich and warming and is lovely served with coconut or brown rice.

1 Preheat the oven to 160°C fan (350°F/Gas 4). Line a baking dish with two sheets of parchment or foil, or an oven bag.

2 Season the steak well with salt and pepper and place in a large bowl.

3 Add the spring onions, garlic, ginger, sesame oil, soy sauce, five spice, star anise and beef stock to the bowl and mix everything together.

4 Slice the mushrooms in half, leaving any little ones whole. Add these to the beef and spices and mix gently together. Tip everything into the lined baking dish, then fold up the parcel tightly (see pages 10–11). (If using an oven bag, snip a few slits in the top to allow steam to escape.)

5 Bake in the oven for 2 hours, until the steak is tender. Give it a good mix around, then garnish with the chillies, cashews and spring onions and serve alongside some fluffy rice.

800g (1lb 12oz) stewing steak, cut into 2-cm (¾-in) pieces
5 spring onions (scallions), finely sliced
2 garlic cloves, grated
3-cm (1¼-in) piece of fresh ginger, grated
2 tbsp sesame oil
2 tbsp light soy sauce
½ tbsp Chinese five spice
4 whole star anise
150ml (⅔ cup) beef stock
150g (5½oz) fresh shiitake mushrooms
salt and freshly ground black pepper

To serve
2 bird's eye chillies, finely sliced
a handful of cashews, toasted and chopped
5 spring onions (scallions), finely sliced
coconut or brown rice

Serves 4

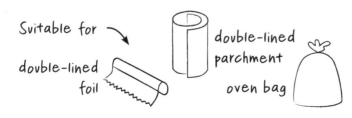

Suitable for

double-lined foil

double-lined parchment

oven bag

Pesto pork with summer vegetables

This is a great recipe to cook when you have friends round. It's heavy on the vegetables, so you'll definitely get most of your five-a-day in this meal alone.

1 Preheat the oven to 190°C fan (410°F/Gas 6–7). Line a baking dish with parchment or foil, or an oven bag.

2 Use a pestle and mortar to crush the basil, pine nuts, Parmesan and garlic together, or pulse in a small food blender. Season with salt and pepper then slowly add the oil and keep crushing until you have a rough pesto.

3 In a large bowl, season the pork then mix in the pesto, ensuring each piece of meat is well covered. Tip into the lined baking dish and fold up the parcel (see pages 10–11). Bake for 25 minutes. (If using an oven bag, snip a few slits in the top to allow steam to escape.)

4 Meanwhile, mix the courgette slices, asparagus and green beans in a bowl with the lemon zest and juice, olive oil and a generous pinch of salt and pepper. Set aside.

5 Pour boiling water over the frozen peas and set aside.

6 After the pork has had 25 minutes, carefully open up the parcel and tip in the vegetables (except for the peas), close up the parcel and return to the oven for 10–15 minutes.

7 Remove the pork and veg from the oven. Drain the peas and add them to the parcel. Stir everything together then tip out onto a big platter to serve.

1 small bunch of basil, leaves and stalks roughly chopped
1 tbsp pine nuts
2 tbsp freshly grated Parmesan
1 garlic clove
1½ tbsp olive oil
600g (1lb 5oz) pork fillet, trimmed of fat and sinew and cut into 2-cm (¾-in) thick medallions
salt and freshly ground black pepper

For the veg
1 medium courgette (zucchini), thickly sliced
200g (7oz) asparagus, trimmed and halved lengthways
200g (7oz) green beans, trimmed
zest and juice of 1 lemon
1 tbsp olive oil
100g (⅔ cup) frozen peas
salt and freshly ground black pepper

Serves 4–6

Svitable for →

foil

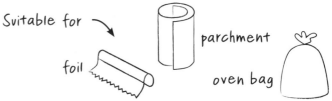

parchment

oven bag

Greek chicken with feta and Kalamata olives

Crispy chicken skin is my guilty pleasure and chicken thighs are, in my opinion, the tastiest part of the bird. This is a great one-pot meal – serve it with a simple, crisp green salad if you want more veg.

1 Preheat the oven to 190°C fan (410°F/Gas 6–7). Line a baking dish with parchment or foil, or an oven bag.

2 Toss the potatoes with 1 tablespoon of the olive oil and some salt in a bowl, then tip into the lined baking dish. Season the chicken thighs with salt and pepper, rub on the remaining olive oil and sprinkle over the dried herbs. Sit the chicken on top of the potatoes, close up the parcel (see pages 10–11) and cook in the oven for 40 minutes. (If using an oven bag, snip a few slits in the top to allow steam to escape.)

3 Carefully open up the parcel, throw in the crumbled feta, olives, cherry tomatoes and red wine vinegar and return to the oven, uncovered, for a further 40 minutes, until the potatoes are tender and the chicken is cooked through (test by inserting a skewer into each thigh and checking the juices run clear). Remove from the oven and serve immediately with some scattered oregano leaves and lemon wedges.

400g (14oz) waxy new
  potatoes, halved
2 tbsp olive oil
4 chicken thighs, skin on
1½ tsp dried oregano
1½ tsp dried thyme
200g (7oz) feta, crumbled
80g (⅔ cup) pitted
  Kalamata olives
150g (5½oz) cherry tomatoes
1 tbsp red wine vinegar
salt and freshly ground
  black pepper

To serve
a few fresh oregano leaves
lemon wedges

Serves 2

Suitable for

foil

parchment

oven bag

Pork belly with cannellini beans

This is a lovely recipe for the winter months when you want something warm and nourishing to eat. It takes over an hour to cook so it needs to go on as soon as you get home from work, but once it's in the oven you can relax. Simply double the recipe to serve four.

1 Preheat the oven to 160°C fan (350°F/Gas 4). Line a baking dish with two sheets of parchment or foil, or an oven bag.

2 Pat the pork belly dry with kitchen paper, score the skin with a sharp knife and slice into 2-cm (¾-in) thick slices. Season all over with salt and pepper.

3 Put the garlic bulb, fennel slices, onion, rosemary, thyme, chicken stock and cider into the lined baking dish. Season with salt and pepper and sit the pork pieces on top, skin side up. Seal the parcel, transfer to the oven to cook for 1 hour. (If using an oven bag, snip a few slits in the top to allow steam to escape.)

4 Open up the parcel, roll down the sides and stir in the beans. Reposition the pork belly so it is skin side up; you want the skin to crisp up during the next period in the oven. Return to the oven, uncovered, and bake for a further 30 minutes, then remove the pork belly and set aside somewhere warm to rest.

5 Squeeze the garlic from the bottom of the bulb so the soft garlic cloves squash out into the beans. Take care not to let any garlic skin drop into the dish, then discard the skins. Gently mix everything together, stir in the kale and return to the oven, uncovered, for another 5 minutes until the kale has wilted.

6 Divide the pork belly slices, beans and vegetables between two warmed plates and sprinkle with the fennel fronds.

400g (14oz) pork belly joint, on the bone
1 whole garlic bulb
1 fennel bulb, trimmed and cut into 5-mm (¼-in) slices, fronds reserved
1 medium onion, thickly sliced
2 sprigs of rosemary
2 sprigs of thyme
250ml (generous 1 cup) chicken stock
100ml (generous ⅓ cup) dry (hard) cider
1 x 400-g (14-oz) can cannellini beans, drained and rinsed
100g (3½oz) curly kale, finely shredded
salt and freshly ground pepper

Serves 2

Suitable for
double-lined foil
double-lined parchment
oven bag

Roast chicken with fennel

I love roast chicken and this is a fabulous way to cook a whole one. You will end up with the juiciest chicken breast ever. The anchovies salt the bird and resulting juices and the fennel ends up soft and slightly chewy at the edges where it meets the parcel walls. This is great served with the Warm potato salad on page 23 and some green beans on the side.

1 Preheat the oven to 200°C fan (425°F/Gas 7). Line a roasting tin with two sheets of parchment or foil, or an oven bag (big enough to completely enclose the chicken).

2 Arrange the fennel slices in a single layer in the lined roasting tin. Sit the chicken on top and season with salt and pepper. Stab the lemon a few times, then push it into the cavity of the chicken.

3 Mix the butter with the thyme leaves, Dijon mustard and some salt and pepper in a small bowl. Lift up the skin at the bottom of each breast and gently push your fingers through to create a space between the skin and the flesh. Push the butter mixture under the skin of the breast and thighs and then add the anchovies in the same way. Take care not to tear the skin.

4 Seal up the parcel (see pages 10–11) and bake for 1 hour (if using an oven bag, snip a few slits in the top to allow steam to escape). Then open up the parcel and return to the oven, uncovered, for another 30 minutes to finish cooking and to brown the skin.

5 Check the chicken is fully cooked by inserting a skewer into the thickest part of the thigh to see if the juices run clear. Or you could use a cook's thermometer (it should read at least 75°C/165°F).

6 Slice and serve the chicken with some of the caramelised fennel and juices.

1 fennel bulb, cut into
   1-cm (½-in) slices
1 x 1.3–1.5-kg (3–3-lb 5-oz)
   whole chicken
1 lemon
20g (1½ tbsp) butter, softened
a few sprigs of thyme, leaves
   picked
1 tbsp Dijon mustard
8 anchovy fillets in oil
olive oil
salt and freshly ground
   black pepper

Serves 4

Suitable for

double-lined foil

double-lined parchment

oven bag

Shin of beef with ale and port

This recipe takes a while in the oven but requires minimal preparation and is a good choice for a lazy weekend. You can pop it in the oven and forget all about it until the timer goes off 5 hours later. It's excellent served with a crisp, buttery baked potato and some simple steamed greens. I have suggested a boneless shin of beef but you can happily add in the bone for extra flavour while cooking.

1 Preheat the oven to 150°C fan (340°F/Gas 3–4). Line a baking dish with two sheets of parchment or foil, or an oven bag.

2 Season the beef generously with salt and pepper and set aside.

3 Put the carrots and onions into the lined baking dish. Add the mushrooms then set the beef shin on top. Mix the tomato purée with the Guinness and port and pour over the top. Tuck in the bay leaves and thyme sprigs.

4 Seal up the parcel tightly (see pages 10–11) and bake in the oven for 5 hours. (If using an oven bag, snip a few slits in the top to allow steam to escape.)

5 Once the cooking time is up, open the parcel and tip everything into a warmed serving dish. Break up the meat with a pair of forks, mix the vegetables and any liquid into the meat and then serve.

1.5kg (3lb 5oz) boneless shin of beef, cut into 2 equal pieces, sinew and hard fat removed
2 large carrots, peeled and cut into 2-cm (¾-in) rounds
2 medium onions, cut into 1-cm (½-in) wedges
10g (⅓oz) dried mushrooms (wild or porcini), soaked in hot water and drained
2 tbsp tomato purée (paste)
500ml (generous 2 cups) Guinness or dark ale
200ml (scant ¾ cup) Tawny port
2 bay leaves
a few sprigs of thyme
salt and freshly ground black pepper

Serves 4

Suitable for

double-lined foil

double-lined parchment

oven bag

Jamaican chicken with rice and peas

This is for spice lovers only as it'll blow your socks off! If you want to dial down the heat, reduce to one Scotch Bonnet or replace with the same quantity of a milder chilli. This recipe is very good served with some natural yogurt on the side to cool down those taste buds.

1 First make the marinade. Blend all the ingredients in a food processor, or in a bowl with a stick blender, until smooth.

2 Score the skin of the chicken thighs in several places with a sharp knife and lay them in a shallow bowl. Pour over the marinade and rub into each chicken thigh. Set aside for at least an hour or, better still, overnight in the fridge to marinate.

3 About an hour before you are ready to eat, preheat the oven to 180°C fan (400°F/Gas 6). Prepare four sheets of parchment or foil, or oven bags.

4 Mix the rice, coconut milk and frozen peas together in a bowl, then divide between the parcels. Arrange two chicken thighs, skin side up, on the top of each parcel. Close up the parcels and bake for 45 minutes. (If using an oven bag, snip a few slits in the top to allow steam to escape.)

5 Open up the parcels, exposing the chicken skins, and bake for another 15 minutes to crisp up the skin. Remove from the oven and check that each piece of chicken is cooked through – the juices should run clear when pierced with a knife.

6 Serve straight onto plates with lime on the side to squeeze over.

8 chicken thighs, skin on
2 x 250-g (9-oz) packets
  pre-cooked brown rice
150ml (²/₃ cup) coconut milk
300g (2 cups) frozen peas
2 limes, halved, to serve

For the jerk marinade
8 spring onions (scallions),
  roughly sliced
1 large shallot, chopped
1 tbsp fresh thyme leaves
2-cm (¾-in) piece of fresh
  ginger, chopped
4 garlic cloves, chopped
2 Scotch Bonnet peppers
1 tbsp fresh thyme leaves
½ tbsp ground allspice
½ tbsp ground black pepper
a few gratings of nutmeg
2 tbsp soft dark brown sugar
1 tbsp light soy sauce
2 tbsp olive oil
2 tbsp red wine vinegar
2 tsp salt

Serves 4

Suitable for

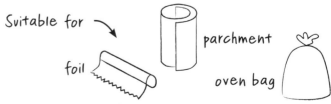

foil

parchment

oven bag

Spicy Szechuan beef with peppers

Szechuan pepper is fruity and very spicy. It packs a punch in this dish, so if you are feeling timid, just add 1 teaspoon instead of ½ tablespoon. I've used sirloin steak here but rump would work well too if you want to save the pennies.

1 Preheat the oven to 200°C fan (425°F/Gas 7). Line a baking dish with parchment or foil, or an oven bag.

2 First make the marinade – mix all the ingredients together in a bowl. Drop in the steak strips, mix well and leave to marinate for at least an hour.

3 In another bowl, mix the vegetables and noodles with the sunflower oil, soy sauce and a pinch of salt. Set aside.

4 Mix the marinated beef with the vegetables and noodles and tip into the lined baking dish. Pour over the beef stock, close up the parcel and bake in the oven for 20 minutes. (If using an oven bag, snip a few slits in the top to allow steam to escape.)

5 Remove from the oven and gently mix everything together again. Scatter over the spring onions and serve immediately.

2 sirloin steaks, approx. 500g (1lb 2oz) total weight, trimmed of fat and cut into 1-cm (½-in) strips
1 red (bell) pepper, deseeded and cut into thin strips
1 yellow (bell) pepper, deseeded and cut into thin strips
a small handful of mangetout (snow peas)
a small handful of baby corn, halved lengthways
300g (10½oz) cooked medium egg or rice noodles
2 tbsp sunflower oil
2 tbsp dark soy sauce
150ml (⅔ cup) hot beef stock
2 spring onions (scallions), sliced
salt

For the marinade
1 tbsp rice vinegar
½ tbsp ground Szechuan pepper
2 tsp dark soy sauce
½ tsp Chinese five spice
2 garlic cloves, crushed
2-cm (¾-in) piece of fresh ginger, finely chopped
1 tsp dried chilli flakes

Serves 2–3

Suitable for

foil

parchment

oven bag

Sausages with sweetcorn, peppers and courgettes

This is such an easy midweek supper, and the addition of passata creates a yummy tomato sauce, so there's no need for ketchup (but if you're like me you'll have ketchup with anything…). If you want to bulk up the meal, boil a pan of new potatoes during the last 10 minutes or serve with a loaf of crusty bread. Minimal fuss.

1 Preheat the oven to 180°C fan (400°F/Gas 6). Line a baking dish with parchment or foil.

2 Mix the onion, peppers, courgette, sweetcorn and olives together in a bowl. Season with salt and pepper then add the za'atar and pour over the olive oil, vinegar and passata. Stir together, then tip into the lined baking dish in a flat-ish layer.

3 Sit the sausages on top then close up the parcel (see pages 10–11) and bake in the oven for 30 minutes.

4 Open up the parcel and return to the oven for another 20 minutes to add some colour and flavour to the sausages and vegetables.

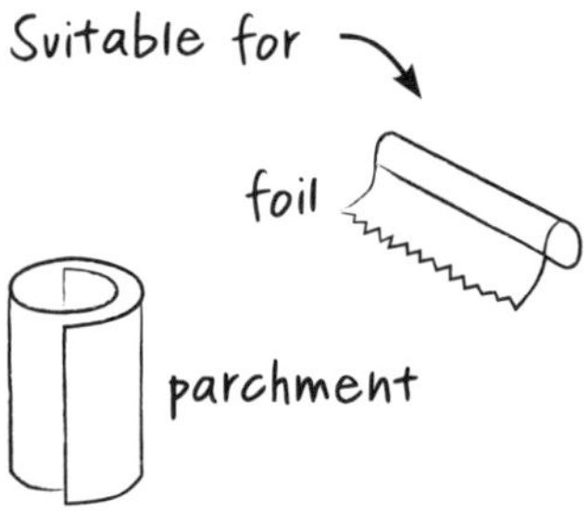

1 red onion, thickly sliced
1 yellow (bell) pepper, deseeded and cut into thick rounds
1 red (bell) pepper, deseeded and cut into thick rounds
1 courgette (zucchini), cut into 1-cm (½-in) slices
198-g (7-oz) can sweetcorn, drained
60g (½ cup) black pitted olives
1 tbsp za'atar
1 tbsp olive oil
1 tbsp balsamic vinegar
100ml (generous ⅓ cup) passata
8 Cumberland sausages
salt and freshly ground black pepper

Serves 4

Suitable for

foil

parchment

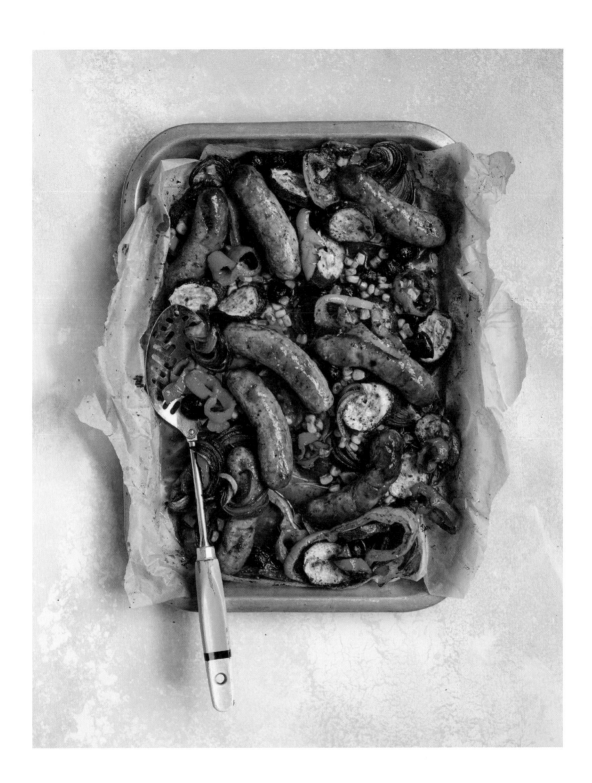

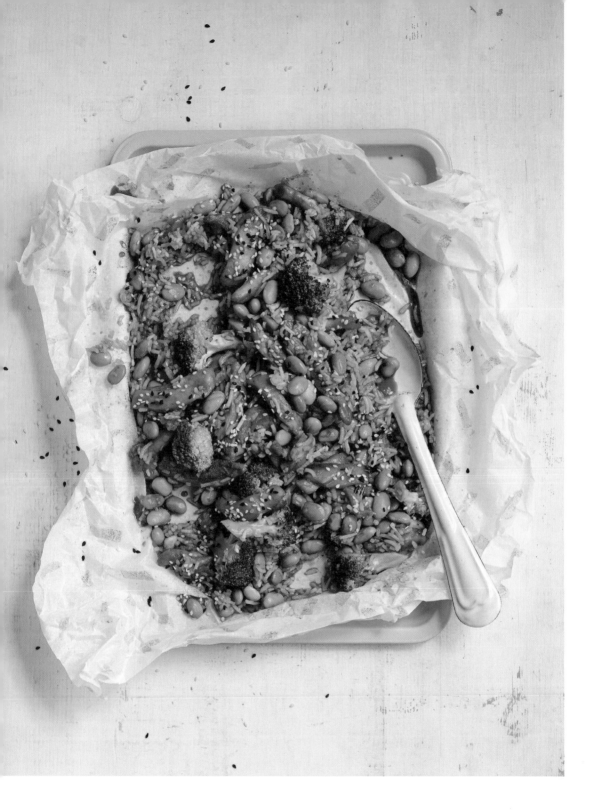

Teriyaki chicken with edamame beans

This recipe makes lots of sauce which gets soaked up by the vegetables and rice in the last stage of cooking, and makes for a really delicious meal. This is a good one-pot, midweek dinner as it takes very little effort and is ready within the hour. Make sure all of your broccoli florets are the same size to ensure even cooking.

1 Preheat the oven to 200°C fan (425°F/Gas 7). Line a baking dish with parchment or foil, or an oven bag.

2 Mix the honey, soy sauce, mirin, vinegar, ginger, garlic and sesame oil together in a large bowl. Add the chicken strips and make sure each piece is well covered. Tip into the lined baking dish, close up the parcel (see pages 10–11) and bake in the oven for 30 minutes. (If using an oven bag, snip a few slits in the top to allow steam to escape.)

3 Remove from the oven, open up the parcel and add the edamame beans, broccoli florets and rice. Stir together to ensure everything is covered and return to the oven, uncovered, for another 15 minutes.

4 Spoon onto warmed plates and serve with a sprinkling of sesame seeds.

2 tbsp runny honey
4 tbsp light soy sauce
4 tbsp mirin
2 tbsp rice wine vinegar
5-cm (2-in) piece of fresh ginger, peeled and grated
1 garlic clove, crushed
2 tbsp sesame oil
600g (1lb 5oz) chicken thigh fillets, cut into 1-cm (½-in) strips
200g (7oz) frozen edamame beans
½ small head broccoli, cut into evenly sized florets
1 x 250-g (9-oz) packet cooked jasmine or basmati rice

To serve
1 tbsp sesame seeds

Serves 4

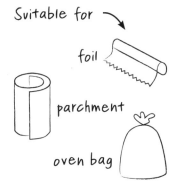

Suitable for

foil

parchment

oven bag

Miso pork with spring vegetables

This dish takes no time at all to prepare and gives you lovely large medallions of pork. All the peas are blanched in boiling water and added at the end of cooking, so they have a good bite. If you'd like to add in some carbohydrates, I'd suggest you serve this with a large bowl of steamed jasmine rice.

1 Preheat the oven to 190°C fan (410°F/Gas 6–7). Line a baking dish with parchment or foil, or an oven bag.

2 Slice the pork fillet into 2-cm (¾-in) thick medallions, season with salt and pepper and put in a bowl along with the miso paste, ginger, sesame oil, honey, rice vinegar and sesame seeds. Mix everything together thoroughly.

3 Tip the pork and sauce into the lined baking dish in a single layer then close up the parcel (see pages 10–11) and bake in the oven for 20 minutes. (If using an oven bag, snip a few slits in the top to allow steam to escape.)

4 Meanwhile, place the mangetout, sugar snap peas and frozen peas in a bowl and cover with boiling water. Set aside.

5 Remove the pork from the oven, open up the parcel and add the asparagus. Close up the parcel again and return to the oven for another 10 minutes.

6 Drain the mangetout and peas then open up the parcel and scatter them over the pork. Serve with a wedge of lime and a sprinkling of coriander leaves.

400g (14oz) pork fillet, fat and sinew trimmed off
1 tbsp brown miso paste
2-cm (¾-in) piece of fresh ginger, grated
½ tbsp sesame oil
½ tbsp runny honey
½ tbsp rice vinegar
1 tbsp sesame seeds
50g (1¾oz) mangetout (snow peas)
50g (1¾oz) sugar snap peas, halved lengthways
100g (⅔ cup) frozen peas
200g (7oz) asparagus, trimmed and halved lengthways

To serve
1 lime, cut into wedges
a small handful of coriander (cilantro) leaves

Serves 2–3

Suitable for

foil

parchment

oven bag / Stasher bag

Paella

I travelled around Spain for a year back in my twenties and I'd have paella as often as possible. This is a simplified version which I've perfected over the years following that trip. It's best made in an oven bag due to the amount of stock needed but you could do it in triple-lined foil – just make sure the sheets are very large so the liquid doesn't seep out of the sides.

1 Preheat the oven to 190°C fan (410°F/Gas 6–7). Line a deep baking dish with three sheets of foil, or an oven bag.

2 Place the onion, garlic, chorizo, bay leaf and chicken strips in the lined baking dish. Drizzle over a little olive oil and season with salt and pepper. Mix everything together and bake, uncovered, for 25 minutes.

3 Mix the rice, saffron and smoked paprika in a bowl then cover with the hot stock. Once the chicken and vegetables have had 25 minutes, give everything a good stir then add the rice and stock to the parcel, season with salt and pepper and stir everything together again. Place the pepper strips on top then close up the parcel. Return to the oven for 20 minutes. (If using an oven bag, snip a few slits in the top to allow steam to escape.)

4 Open up the parcel, add the prawns, squid and peas and stir gently, then return the parcel to the oven, uncovered, for another 10 minutes. Remove from the oven and leave to stand for 5 minutes. Serve with chopped parsley and a generous squeeze of lemon juice.

Suitable for → triple-lined foil / oven bag

1 medium onion, finely chopped
1 garlic clove, finely chopped
120g (4¼oz) cooking chorizo, finely chopped
1 bay leaf
600g (1lb 5oz) skinless, boneless chicken thighs, sliced into strips
olive oil, for drizzling
300g (generous 1½ cups) paella rice
a pinch of saffron
1 tsp hot smoked paprika
500ml (generous 2 cups) hot chicken or vegetable stock
4 piquillo peppers from a jar, sliced into strips
100g (3½oz) raw shell-on king prawns (jumbo shrimp), shells removed but heads kept on
200g (7oz) baby squid, cleaned, quills and beaks removed and cut into ½-cm (¼-in) rings, tentacles separated
100g (⅔ cup) frozen peas
salt and freshly ground black pepper

To serve
flat leaf parsley, roughly chopped
lemon wedges

Serves 6

DESSERTS

Roasted rhubarb with vanilla, orange and cinnamon

Rhubarb cooked in this way is one of my favourite dishes. It's best made with forced rhubarb in the late winter months, as the stems tend to be paler in colour and more delicate in flavour. Summer rhubarb is fine, but it may need a little more sugar, as it is sharper, and a longer cooking time.

1 Preheat the oven to 160°C fan (350°F/Gas 4). Line a baking dish with parchment or foil.

2 Cut the rhubarb into about 4-cm (1½in) lengths and arrange in the lined baking dish in single layer. Dot the vanilla bean paste over the top, add the orange zest and pour over the juice. Tuck the cinnamon stick in and sprinkle over the sugar.

3 Carefully close up the parcel (see pages 10–11), taking care not to disturb the layer of rhubarb, and bake for 20 minutes, until the rhubarb is tender but not collapsed. It may need another 5 minutes to soften up but it can collapse very quickly, so keep an eye on it!

4 Serve with rich dark chocolate ice cream.

400g (14oz) thin sticks rhubarb
1 tsp vanilla bean paste
1 piece of pared orange zest and juice of 1 orange
1 cinnamon stick
2 tbsp caster (superfine) sugar

To serve
dark chocolate ice cream

Serves 2–3

Suitable for
foil
parchment

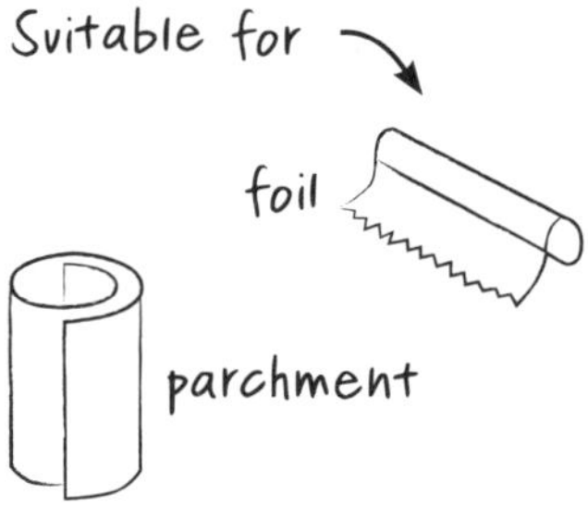

Banana, chocolate and peanut butter sundae

I was about seven years old when I was first given this to eat and I thought I had landed in heaven – hot squishy banana with molten chocolate and a pile of ice cream. Use squirty cream if you're in a retro mood. This recipe works just as well cooked on a barbecue.

1 Preheat the oven to 160°C fan (350°F/Gas 4). Line a baking dish with parchment or foil.

2 Leaving the skin on, slice the banana deeply down the middle lengthways. Sit the banana on the foil or parchment and gently prise it open. Stuff in the chocolate chips and pile on the peanut butter. Fold the parcel up around the banana (see pages 10–11) and bake in the oven for 20 minutes.

3 Remove the banana from the oven, open up the parcel and pile on the vanilla ice cream, whipped double cream and glacé cherries, and top with chocolate sprinkles. Go mad! Eat immediately with childish abandon.

1 banana
30g (1oz) chocolate chips
1 tbsp crunchy peanut butter
1 large scoop vanilla ice cream
60ml (¼ cup) double (heavy) cream, whipped
2 glacé cherries, halved
chocolate sprinkles, to decorate

Makes 1, but doubles, triples and quadruples easily depending on how many mouths there are to feed! Use a separate piece of parchment or foil for each serving.

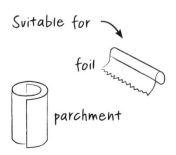

Suitable for
foil
parchment

Boozy Bourbon baked apples with maple syrup and sultanas

Bourbon is my poison, and these apples remind me of autumn, open fires and big cosy jumpers. Best eaten in front of the telly with a large scoop of ice cream on the side.

1 Preheat the oven to 180°C fan (400°F/Gas 6). Line a baking dish with two large pieces of foil or parchment, one horizontal and the other vertical.

2 Pour the Bourbon over the sultanas in a small bowl and set aside to soak.

3 Core the apples and score a line around each circumference – this will help stop the apples from bursting.

4 Mix the sugar, butter, spices, maple syrup and lemon zest together in a bowl. Strain the sultanas, reserving the Bourbon, and mix the fruit into the butter mixture.

5 Arrange the cored apples in the middle of the lined baking dish and stuff the butter mixture into each core. Pour over the reserved Bourbon, fold up the parcel so it is tightly sealed (see pages 10–11) and bake for 50 minutes.

6 Allow to stand for a couple of minutes before serving with the ice cream. The apples will be lovely and soft with lots of delicious syrup.

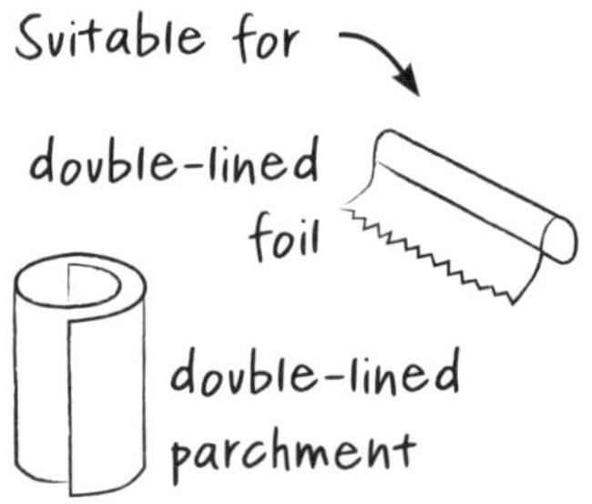

2 tbsp Bourbon
50g (scant ½ cup) sultanas
4 Granny Smith or
    Braeburn apples
1 tbsp soft light brown sugar
50g (3½ tbsp) soft butter
1 tsp ground cinnamon
¼ tsp ground nutmeg
2 tbsp maple syrup
zest of ½ lemon

To serve
vanilla ice cream

Serves 4

Suitable for

double-lined foil

double-lined parchment

Poached pears with hidden chocolate sauce

These are fun to make and lots of chocolate sauce is created to make pools around each pear. They are cooked individually in their own parchment and it's nice for each person to unwrap their own pear so they get to discover the hidden chocolate sauce for themselves.

1 Preheat the oven to 180°C fan (400°F/Gas 6). Prepare four squares of parchment or foil, big enough to wrap around each pear.

2 Core the pears with an apple corer almost all the way through from the bottom up, keeping the stalk and top of the pear intact. Squeeze over the lemon juice to prevent them from browning and set aside.

3 In a small bowl, mix together the lemon zest, vanilla bean paste, butter, muscovado sugar and dark chocolate. Turn the pears upside down and stuff this mixture into the cavity. You will need to push down to fit all the ingredients in.

4 Turn the pears the right way up and sit them onto the individual squares of parchment or foil. Sprinkle 1 teaspoon of caster sugar over each pear. Scrunch up the parcels carefully but tightly. It's fine for the stalk to peep out at the top. Sit the parcels in a baking dish and bake for 40–45 minutes, until soft and yielding but still holding their shape. A chocolate sauce will have formed around the base of each pear.

5 Serve each pear, still in its parcel, in bowls with some double cream on the side.

4 ripe but firm pears, peeled
zest and juice of ½ lemon
½ tsp vanilla bean paste
20g (1½ tbsp) unsalted
  butter, softened
2 tbsp dark muscovado sugar
40g (1½oz) dark chocolate,
  roughly chopped
4 tsp caster (superfine) sugar

To serve
double (heavy) cream

Serves 4

Suitable for
foil
parchment

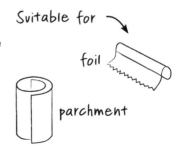

Pineapple en papillote with rum

Pina colada in pudding form anyone? It's literally impossible to have any leftovers of this dish as it *has* to be scoffed all in one go. Warm juicy pineapple with a sticky sugary sauce and boozy cream… gosh! Why not serve this with an actual pina colada?! Make sure you choose a ripe pineapple and you will be rewarded with every bite.

1 Preheat the oven to 200°C fan (425°F/Gas 7). Lay a large piece of foil onto a baking dish and top with a large piece parchment.

2 Arrange the pineapple wedges on the parchment in a single layer. Dot over the vanilla bean paste and butter and sprinkle over the sugar and half of the rum. Mix everything together with your hands to coat all the pineapple wedges.

3 Fold and seal the parchment and foil parcel (see pages 10–11) and bake in the oven for 15 minutes, then open up the parcel, baste the pineapple wedges with the juices and roast, uncovered, for a further 20 minutes.

4 Softly whip the cream until it just holds its shape, then stir in the remaining rum. Serve the pineapple pieces with the cooking juices poured over, a dollop of rum cream and a scattering of macadamia nuts.

1 large ripe pineapple, peeled, "eyes" removed and cut into 6 long wedges
1 tsp vanilla bean paste
50g (3½ tbsp) butter, cut into pieces
50g (¼ cup) light muscovado sugar
2 tbsp dark rum
150ml (⅔ cup) double (heavy) cream
50g (1¾oz) macadamia nuts, toasted and roughly chopped

Serves 4–6

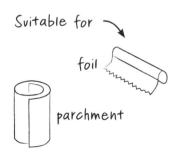

Suitable for

foil

parchment

Honey-roasted fruit with pistachios and Greek yogurt

A colourful dish of spiced fruit with clusters of grapes, this is very simple indeed and is delicious eaten warm or cold. You could swap in pecans, almonds or walnuts for the pistachios if you prefer. This is also lovely for breakfast the following day with muesli or granola and yogurt.

1 Preheat the oven to 180°C fan (400°F/Gas 6). Line a baking dish with parchment or foil.

2 Cut the plums into quarters, remove the stone, and halve the figs. Keep the grapes on the vine but separate them into smaller clusters. Place the fruit in the lined baking dish and drizzle with the honey. Tuck in the cinnamon stick and orange zest and scatter over the stem ginger slices. Squeeze over the orange juice.

3 Close up the parcel (see pages 10–11) and bake for 30–40 minutes, until the fruit has softened and burst a little.

4 Serve the warm fruit and juices with the chopped pistachios and a dollop of Greek yogurt.

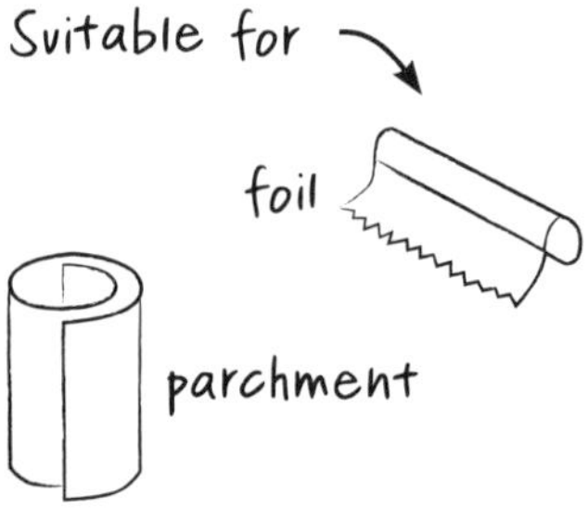

4 ripe plums
4 ripe black figs
150g (5½oz) black grapes (Sable are best if you can get hold of them)
2 tbsp runny orange blossom honey
1 cinnamon stick
pared zest and juice of 1 orange
1 ball of preserved stem ginger, sliced

To serve
a small handful of pistachios, roughly chopped
Greek yogurt

Serves 4

Suitable for

foil

parchment

Maple chocolate strawberries

This is a lovely way to eat strawberries and is also delicious the following day spooned over your morning porridge – if you're going to do this, though, omit the chocolate chips and add them to the porridge while it's cooking – pure indulgence.

1 Preheat the oven to 190°C fan (410°F/Gas 6–7). Line a baking dish with parchment or foil.

2 Cut any larger strawberries in half but keep the smallish ones whole and sit them in the lined baking dish. Dot over the vanilla bean paste and maple syrup and add the star anise and black peppercorns. Mix everything together then seal up the parcel (see pages 10–11) and bake in the oven for 15–20 minutes.

3 Remove the dish from the oven, open up the parcel and scatter over the chocolate chips and pistachios. Allow the chocolate to melt around the hot strawberries, then serve immediately with some Greek yogurt on the side.

400g (14oz) ripe strawberries, hulls removed
½ tsp vanilla bean paste
4 tbsp maple syrup
1 whole star anise
6 whole black peppercorns
30g (1oz) dark chocolate chips
a small handful of pistachios, roughly chopped

To serve
Greek yogurt

Serves 3

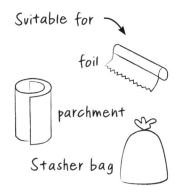

Suitable for

foil

parchment

Stasher bag

Stewed plums with star anise

I'm a big fan of cooking fruit with whole spices and anything with an aniseed flavour will be top of my list. Star anise goes well with plums in this sweet dish but it's not overpowering and the almond extract is delicate but still prominent. You'll get some lovely purple juices, too. I've suggested you serve this with Greek yogurt but it's also delicious with vanilla ice cream.

1 Preheat the oven to 190°C fan (410°F/Gas 6–7). Line a baking dish with parchment or foil, or an oven bag.

2 Put the plums, cut side up, into the lined baking dish. Drizzle over the honey, orange juice and almond extract. Add the star anise. Close up the parcel (see pages 10–11) and bake in the oven for 15 minutes. (If using an oven bag, snip a few slits in the top to allow steam to escape.)

3 Open up the parcel, sprinkle over the flaked almonds and return to the oven, uncovered, for 5–10 minutes.

4 Serve warm with Greek yogurt.

6 ripe plums, halved, stones removed
1 tbsp runny honey
juice of 1 orange
¼ tsp almond extract
2 whole star anise
2 tbsp flaked (slivered) almonds

To serve
Greek yogurt

Serves 4

Suitable for

foil

parchment

oven bag /
Stasher bag

Coconut and ginger rice pudding with mangoes

A good rice pudding is hard to beat. This is my Chinese-inspired version. When visiting my best friend while she was living in Hong Kong, we'd go out to pudding bars to eat dessert (why don't we have pudding bars in the UK?!) and cold coconut rice with mangoes was always on the menu. This is a warmed-up version that is yummy as a breakfast or pudding.

1 Preheat the oven to 160°C fan (350°F/Gas 4). Line a baking dish with parchment or foil, or an oven bag.

2 Mix the rice, coconut cream, sugar, stem ginger and syrup together in a bowl and tip into the lined baking dish. Tuck in the lime leaf, then close up the parcel (see pages 10–11) and bake for 20 minutes. (If using an oven bag, snip a few slits in the top to allow steam to escape.)

3 Remove from the oven, top with the sliced mango and toasted coconut flakes and squeeze over the lime juice to serve.

1 x 250-g (9-oz) packet pre-cooked basmati rice
200ml (scant ¾ cup) coconut cream
1 tbsp soft light brown sugar
1 ball of preserved stem ginger, finely chopped
1 tbsp preserved stem ginger syrup
1 lime leaf, fresh if possible

To serve
2 ripe mangoes, sliced
dried coconut flakes, toasted
juice of 1 lime

Serves 2

Suitable for

foil

parchment

oven bag / Stasher bag

Berry crumble

Frozen berries make great crumbles and can be cooked straight from the freezer. I've used spelt flour here but you could easily use plain flour instead. The crumble topping is meant to be loose so it will soak up the juices from the fruit bubbling beneath it.

1 Preheat the oven to 190°C fan (410°F/Gas 6–7). Line a deep baking dish with two sheets of foil or an oven bag.

2 Mix the berries, lemon zest and juice and the brown sugar together in a bowl. Spoon into the the lined baking dish and close up the parcel (if using an oven bag, snip a few slits in the top to allow steam to escape). Bake in the oven for 10 minutes – the berries will still be whole but some juices will start to form.

3 Meanwhile, in another large bowl, mix the flour with the cinnamon and ground cardamom. Rub in the butter then stir in the sugar, oats and pecans. The crumble will have a sandy texture.

4 Open up the parcel and roll down the sides to expose as much of the berries as possible. Pour over the crumble topping, taking care not to pack it down too tightly: you want it loose. Return the parcel to the oven, uncovered, for a further 25–30 minutes, until the topping is golden brown.

5 Serve with lots of double cream.

1kg (2lb 4oz) frozen summer berries (raspberries, redcurrants, blackberries)
zest and juice of 1 lemon
100g (½ cup) soft light brown sugar

For the topping
150g (generous 1 cup) spelt flour
½ tsp ground cinnamon
a generous pinch of ground cardamom
100g (3½oz) butter, softened
75g (⅓ cup) caster (superfine) sugar
75g (¾ cup) jumbo (old-fashioned) oats
30g (1oz) pecans, chopped

To serve
very thick double (heavy) cream

Serves 6–8

Suitable for

double-lined foil

oven bag

Slow-cooked peaches

These peaches are great served as a pudding or even for breakfast. The cooking time will vary depending on how ripe your peaches are: the harder they are, the more time they will need to cook. They are best made at the height of their season, during the late summer months.

1 Preheat the oven to 160°C fan (350°F/Gas 4). Line a baking dish with parchment or foil, or an oven bag.

2 Place the peach wedges, in a single layer, in the lined baking dish. Tuck in the strips of lemon zest then pour over the Amaretto, honey and 3 tablespoons of water. Close up the parcel (see pages 10–11) and bake in the oven for 45 minutes. (If using an oven bag, snip a few slits in the top to allow steam to escape.)

3 Remove from the oven and take out the lemon zest. Serve the peaches warm, or at room temperature, topped with crushed Amaretti biscuits, chopped pecans and a dollop of crème fraîche.

4 ripe yellow- or white-fleshed peaches, stones removed, sliced into 1-cm (½-in) wedges
pared zest from ½ lemon
3 tbsp Amaretto
2 tbsp runny chestnut or heather honey

To serve
a handful of Amaretti biscuits, crushed
a handful of pecans, roughly chopped
crème fraîche

Serves 4

Suitable for
foil
parchment
oven bag /
Stasher bag

Individual apricot and frangipane tarts

Tangy apricots and buttery almonds are a classic flavour combination. This recipe uses canned apricots, which are inexpensive, but you could easily use fresh apricots when they're in season. These tarts are crustless and gluten-free and you'll definitely want to eat more than one. Great served with coffee.

1 Preheat the oven to 180°C fan (400°F/Gas 6). Brush six ramekins with a little melted butter. Line a small, deep sided baking dish with two sheets of foil or an oven bag, large enough to completely enclose the contents of the tray, and sit the buttered ramekins inside.

2 Mix the melted butter, sugar, ground almonds, egg, cardamom and almond extract together in a bowl until well combined. Spoon the batter evenly into the ramekins and top each with 1–2 apricot halves. They will sink a little.

3 Carefully close up the parcel and bake in the oven for 30 minutes. (If using an oven bag, snip a few slits in the top to allow steam to escape.)

4 Open up the parcel, sprinkle over the flaked almonds and return to the oven, uncovered, for another 10 minutes. The filling should be golden brown and puffed up. If not, return to the oven for another 5 minutes.

5 Remove from the oven and brush with the reserved syrup. Leave to cool for 10 minutes before serving with clotted cream.

100g (3½oz) butter, melted, plus extra for greasing
100g (generous ½ cup) caster (superfine) sugar
100g (1 cup) ground almonds
1 small egg
a pinch of ground cardamom
1–2 drops almond extract
9–12 apricot halves (from 1 x 410-g/14½-oz can apricot halves in light syrup), plus 2 tbsp syrup
1 tbsp flaked (slivered) almonds

To serve
clotted cream

Makes 6 tarts

Suitable for

double-lined foil

oven bag

Chocolate chip steamed cakes

This is my version of a 'Mushi-pan' – a Japanese steamed cake – which is usually made on the stove in a steamer. I've adapted the method for the oven and it makes the most delicious, soft little cakes. Gooey and moreish.

1 Preheat the oven to 160°C fan (350°F/Gas 4). Line four dariole moulds or ramekins with cupcake cases and sit the moulds in an oven bag, resting in a small, deep baking dish.

2 Sift all the dry ingredients together in a bowl, making sure to break up any lumps of brown sugar. In a separate bowl, whisk together the egg, milk and oil. Add the wet ingredients to the dry ingredients and combine, adding a little more milk, if necessary, to create a soft dropping consistency. Fold in half of the chocolate chips

3 Spoon the batter evenly into the paper cases and sprinkle over the remaining chocolate chips. Boil a kettle and carefully pour the hot water into the bag, taking care not to get any water into the cake mixture, until the water is about 1cm (½in) up the sides of the moulds. Close up the bag, leaving room for the air to circulate, and snip a few small slits into the top of the bag to allow steam to escape. Bake for 18–20 minutes, until the cakes have risen and are springy to the touch.

4 Allow a minute or so to cool before turning out of the moulds and serving.

80g (⅔ cup) plain (all-purpose) flour
1 tsp baking powder
1½ tbsp unsweetened cocoa powder
2 tbsp soft dark brown sugar
1 large egg
60ml (¼ cup) milk
2 tbsp sunflower or vegetable oil
60g (2oz) chocolate chips

Makes 4, but can easily be doubled

Suitable for

oven bag

Figs with ricotta, honey and walnuts

Ripe figs are just wonderful: jammy, sweet and best eaten straight off the tree. This recipe is good for a glut and is more of a sweet mouthful than a whole pudding. If your figs aren't quite ripe, cook them for a few minutes longer.

1 Preheat the oven to 180°C fan (400°F/Gas 6). Line a baking dish with parchment or foil.

2 Cut a deep cross in the top of each fig and sit each one upright in the lined baking dish. Add the rosemary sprig and sprinkle over the sugar. Close up the parcel (see pages 10–11) and bake the figs for 20 minutes.

3 Meanwhile, mix the ricotta with the honey and chopped walnuts in a bowl.

4 Remove the figs from the oven and set aside to cool. Once cool, gently prise open the figs, stuff with the ricotta mixture and decorate with a few rosemary needles and an extra drizzle of honey.

8 small ripe figs
1 sprig of rosemary, a few leaves removed to decorate
1 tbsp soft light brown sugar
90g (3¼oz) ricotta
1 tbsp runny honey, plus extra to serve
5–6 walnut halves, finely chopped

Makes 8 stuffed figs

Suitable for

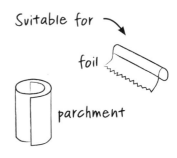

foil

parchment

Sticky steamed ginger puddings

This recipe can easily be doubled to make eight puddings – cook in two bags if you are increasing the quantity. I've suggested serving them with custard but you could easily serve them with stem ginger ice cream. Both would be ludicrously indulgent but life is short, so why not?

1 Preheat the oven to 160°C fan (350°F/Gas 4). Line a deep-sided baking dish with an oven bag.

2 First make the sauce. Mix the butter and sugar together in a small bowl to form a paste then spread evenly inside the bottom and sides of 4 dariole moulds.

3 Next make the puddings. Combine the butter, sugar, flour, vanilla extract, ground ginger and egg together in a bowl and mix with a hand whisk until just combined. Stir in the stem ginger then spoon the mixture into the moulds, smoothing out the top of the mixture.

4 Place the moulds in the oven bag, then bring up the sides of the bag and carefully pour 1cm (½in) of boiling water in between the dariole moulds, taking care not to get any water into the pudding mixture. Seal the bag, leaving plenty of room above the puddings for the air to circulate, and snip a few slits into the top of the bag to allow steam to escape. Place in the oven and bake for 30–35 minutes.

5 When ready, the tops should be springy to touch and the sides will have shrunk away from the sides of the moulds. Remove from the bag and leave to sit for 5 minutes before turning out onto plates, sprinkling with chopped ginger and serving with custard.

For the sauce
40g (3 tbsp) very soft butter
40g (1½oz) soft dark brown sugar

For the puddings
80g (3oz) very soft butter
80g (3oz) soft dark brown sugar
80g (3oz) self-raising flour
1 tsp vanilla extract
1 tsp ground ginger
1 large egg
1 ball preserved stem ginger, finely chopped, plus extra to serve

To serve
custard

Serves 4

Suitable for

oven bag

Nectarines with sweet geranium

I first came across sweet geranium (lemon-scented pelargonium) when I was studying to be a chef in Ireland. The school was nuts about it and I was easily converted, coming home with my own plant to take care of. I am notorious for killing plants but, against all the odds, this plant has thrived in my care! The leaves are lemon-scented and very versatile, so let me know if you want a cutting for your own pots. If you can't find it then replace it with lemon balm, lemon verbena or even a couple of fresh lime leaves.

4 ripe yellow-fleshed
   nectarines
2 tbsp demerara sugar
3–4 sweet geranium leaves

To serve
pine nuts, toasted
clotted cream

Serves 4

1 Preheat the oven to 200°C fan (425°F/Gas 7). Line a baking dish with parchment or foil.

2 Halve the nectarines and remove the stones. Arrange in a single layer, cut side up, in the middle of the lined baking dish. Sprinkle over 1 tablespoon of the sugar and tuck in the sweet geranium leaves. Carefully pour in 3 tablespoons of water, close up the parcel (see pages 10–11) and bake in the oven for 20 minutes. Cook for a little longer if your nectarines are not quite soft enough.

3 Remove from the oven, open up the parcel, sprinkle over the remaining sugar and return to the oven, uncovered, for another 10 minutes. You want the nectarines to be soft but still holding their shape and lightly caramelised on top.

4 Remove from the oven and allow to cool slightly before sprinkling over the toasted pine nuts and serving with a spoonful of clotted cream.

Suitable for

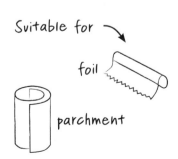

foil

parchment

Index

Acknowledgements

Very many thank yous to these special people:

Harriet and Katherine at Quadrille for commissioning me and for editing and designing this book; Ola, Barbara, Sophie and Evie for making our shoot such fun and for providing wisdom and succour for the upcoming delivery of the baby in my tummy and my second baby, this book! Tonia for the props and all that beautiful hand-printed parchment paper. Thank you also to Sam for her supreme editing skills and for keeping track of all the changes – I don't know how you do it! To my local friends in Battersea who taste-tested each recipe and encouraged me along the way, thank you for being hungry all the time. And to my family and to Chris for being wonderful.